WIRELESS SECURITY MASTERCLASS

PENETRATION TESTING FOR NETWORK DEFENDERS AND ETHICAL HACKERS

4 BOOKS IN 1

BOOK 1
WIRELESS NETWORK SECURITY ESSENTIALS: A BEGINNER'S GUIDE

BOOK 2
HACKING WI-FI NETWORKS: INTERMEDIATE TECHNIQUES FOR PENETRATION TESTERS

BOOK 3
ADVANCED WIRELESS EXPLOITATION: A COMPREHENSIVE GUIDE TO PENETRATION TESTING

BOOK 4
WIRELESS NETWORK MASTERY: EXPERT-LEVEL PENETRATION TESTING AND DEFENSE

ROB BOTWRIGHT

Published by Rob Botwright
Library of Congress Cataloging-in-Publication Data
ISBN 978-1-83938-543-8
Cover design by Rizzo

Disclaimer

The contents of this book are based on extensive research and the best available historical sources. However, the author and publisher make no claims, promises, or guarantees about the accuracy, completeness, or adequacy of the information contained herein. The information in this book is provided on an "as is" basis, and the author and publisher disclaim any and all liability for any errors, omissions, or inaccuracies in the information or for any actions taken in reliance on such information.

The opinions and views expressed in this book are those of the author and do not necessarily reflect the official policy or position of any organization or individual mentioned in this book. Any reference to specific people, places, or events is intended only to provide historical context and is not intended to defame or malign any group, individual, or entity.

The information in this book is intended for educational and entertainment purposes only. It is not intended to be a substitute for professional advice or judgment. Readers are encouraged to conduct their own research and to seek professional advice where appropriate.

Every effort has been made to obtain necessary permissions and acknowledgments for all images and other copyrighted material used in this book. Any errors or omissions in this regard are unintentional, and the author and publisher will correct them in future editions.

TABLE OF CONTENTS – BOOK 1 - WIRELESS NETWORK SECURITY ESSENTIALS: A BEGINNER'S GUIDE

TABLE OF CONTENTS – BOOK 2 - HACKING WI-FI NETWORKS: INTERMEDIATE TECHNIQUES FOR PENETRATION TESTERS

TABLE OF CONTENTS – BOOK 3 - ADVANCED WIRELESS EXPLOITATION: A COMPREHENSIVE GUIDE TO PENETRATION TESTING

TABLE OF CONTENTS – BOOK 4 - WIRELESS NETWORK MASTERY: EXPERT-LEVEL PENETRATION TESTING AND DEFENSE

Introduction

In the fast-paced digital landscape of today, where connectivity is the backbone of modern life, the security of wireless networks has become paramount. As technology advances, so do the threats that target these networks, making it essential for network defenders and ethical hackers to be at the forefront of safeguarding our digital realm. Welcome to the "Wireless Security Masterclass: Penetration Testing for Network Defenders and Ethical Hackers" book bundle.

This comprehensive bundle comprises four meticulously crafted books, each designed to equip readers with the knowledge, skills, and expertise needed to navigate the complex and ever-evolving world of wireless security. Whether you're an absolute beginner seeking to understand the essentials, an intermediate learner eager to delve deeper into Wi-Fi network penetration testing, or an expert aiming to master advanced techniques and defenses, this bundle has something for everyone.

Book 1 - Wireless Network Security Essentials: A Beginner's Guide introduces you to the fundamental concepts of wireless security. It provides a solid foundation for understanding encryption, authentication, and the various security protocols that underpin wireless networks. Designed with beginners in mind, this book ensures that you grasp the essentials before embarking on your journey towards becoming a wireless security expert.

Book 2 - Hacking Wi-Fi Networks: Intermediate Techniques for Penetration Testers takes you to the next level of wireless security exploration. Here, you will explore intermediate-level techniques employed by ethical hackers and penetration testers to uncover vulnerabilities in Wi-Fi networks. Topics include cracking Wi-Fi passwords, conducting wireless reconnaissance, and understanding advanced attacks.

Book 3 - Advanced Wireless Exploitation: A Comprehensive Guide to Penetration Testing delves deep into the intricate world of wireless exploitation. This book equips you with the skills to identify hidden SSIDs, exploit weaknesses in Wi-Fi protocols, and evade intrusion detection systems. It is a comprehensive guide for those seeking to conduct advanced penetration tests on wireless networks.

Book 4 - Wireless Network Mastery: Expert-Level Penetration Testing and Defense is the pinnacle of our journey. In this book, you will explore expert-level penetration testing techniques, advanced network mapping, and the art of exploiting misconfigurations. Additionally, you will learn critical aspects of maintaining persistent access, anti-forensic techniques, and countermeasures for detection and attribution. This book transforms you into a seasoned expert capable of defending against the most sophisticated wireless attacks.

In the pages of this "Wireless Security Masterclass" book bundle, you will find not only knowledge but also empowerment. You will gain the tools and insights needed to secure your own networks, identify vulnerabilities, and contribute to the ongoing mission of making our wireless world a safer place.

As technology continues to evolve and threats persistently adapt, the skills you acquire through this bundle will be invaluable. Whether you're a network defender, an aspiring ethical hacker, or a seasoned expert, the knowledge you gain here will serve as a guiding light in the realm of wireless security.

Welcome to the "Wireless Security Masterclass," where we embark on a journey to master the art of wireless security and ensure the safety of the digital world we all depend on. Let's dive in and explore the boundless possibilities and challenges of wireless security together.

BOOK 1
WIRELESS NETWORK SECURITY ESSENTIALS
A BEGINNER'S GUIDE

ROB BOTWRIGHT

Chapter 1: Introduction to Wireless Networks

Wireless communication forms the backbone of our interconnected world. It's a technology that enables devices to exchange information without the need for physical cables. At its core, wireless communication relies on electromagnetic waves to transmit data through the air. These waves carry information in the form of radio frequency signals.

Understanding the fundamentals of wireless communication is essential for anyone delving into the world of wireless network security. To grasp the intricacies of securing wireless networks, we need to start with the basics. The electromagnetic spectrum plays a crucial role in wireless communication. It encompasses a wide range of frequencies, from radio waves to microwaves, infrared, visible light, ultraviolet, X-rays, and gamma rays. Each part of the spectrum has its unique characteristics and applications. In the context of wireless networks, the radio frequency portion of the electromagnetic spectrum is of primary importance. This is where Wi-Fi, Bluetooth, cellular networks, and other wireless technologies operate. Wireless signals are essentially variations in the electromagnetic field, created by oscillating electrical charges in transmitting antennas. These variations travel through the air and are picked up by receiving antennas, where they are converted back into electrical signals.

Understanding the characteristics of radio waves is essential for optimizing wireless network performance. Factors such as frequency, wavelength, amplitude, and propagation can affect the quality and range of wireless signals.

Frequency, measured in Hertz (Hz), determines the number of oscillations per second in a radio wave. Higher frequencies carry more data but have shorter ranges and can be more easily blocked by obstacles.

Wavelength, on the other hand, is the physical distance between successive peaks or troughs of a wave. It is inversely proportional to frequency, meaning that higher frequencies have shorter wavelengths and vice versa.

Amplitude represents the strength or intensity of a wave, which affects the signal's strength and, to some extent, its range.

Propagation refers to how radio waves travel through space. It can be influenced by factors such as reflection, diffraction, and interference. Understanding propagation helps network engineers design efficient wireless networks.

Now, let's talk about antennas. Antennas are essential components in wireless communication systems. They serve both as transmitters and receivers of electromagnetic waves.

Antennas come in various shapes and sizes, each designed for specific purposes. Omni-directional antennas radiate signals in all directions, making them suitable for providing coverage in a circular area. Directional antennas focus their signals in specific directions, allowing for longer-range communication.

To maximize signal strength and coverage, the placement and orientation of antennas are crucial considerations when setting up wireless networks.

The concept of modulation plays a key role in wireless communication. Modulation involves varying certain properties of the carrier wave, such as its amplitude, frequency, or phase, to encode information.

Different modulation techniques are used in wireless systems to transmit data efficiently. For instance, Amplitude Modulation (AM) varies the signal's amplitude, Frequency Modulation (FM) changes its frequency, and Phase Shift Keying (PSK) alters its phase.

The choice of modulation scheme depends on factors like data rate, signal quality, and available bandwidth. Advanced wireless technologies often employ complex modulation schemes to achieve high data transfer rates.

Wireless communication wouldn't be possible without the use of transceivers. A transceiver is a device that combines both transmitter and receiver functions. It can send and receive signals over the air, facilitating bidirectional communication.

Transceivers are integral components of wireless devices such as smartphones, laptops, and Wi-Fi routers. They allow these devices to connect to wireless networks and communicate with other devices in the vicinity.

Now, let's explore the concept of wireless networks themselves. A wireless network is a collection of interconnected devices that communicate with each other wirelessly. These networks can be as small as a home Wi-Fi network or as large as a cellular network covering an entire city.

Wireless networks rely on access points or base stations to facilitate communication between devices. Access points act as central hubs, providing connectivity and managing data traffic within the network.

One of the most common types of wireless networks is Wi-Fi, short for Wireless Fidelity. Wi-Fi networks use radio waves to transmit data between devices and access points. They are widely used for internet connectivity in homes, businesses, and public places.

The IEEE 802.11 family of standards governs Wi-Fi technology. These standards define the specifications for wireless communication protocols, including data rates, frequency bands, and security features.

Securing Wi-Fi networks is of paramount importance to protect sensitive data and ensure privacy. Wi-Fi security encompasses various measures, including encryption, authentication, and access control.

Wi-Fi encryption protocols like WPA2 and WPA3 help safeguard data by encrypting it before transmission. Authentication mechanisms ensure that only authorized users can access the network.

Access control involves setting up permissions and restrictions to limit who can connect to the network and what they can do once connected.

Understanding the basics of wireless communication sets the foundation for exploring the intricacies of wireless network security. It's a fascinating field that combines technology, engineering, and cybersecurity to ensure the confidentiality and integrity of data transmitted wirelessly.

As we embark on our journey through the historical evolution of wireless technology, we're about to discover a fascinating chronicle of innovation, communication, and human progress. It all began in the late 19th century when inventors like Nikola Tesla and Guglielmo Marconi paved the way for wireless communication by experimenting with electromagnetic waves. Marconi's successful transmission of the first wireless telegraph signals across the Atlantic Ocean in 1901 marked a groundbreaking achievement, ushering in the era of long-distance wireless communication. During the early 20th century, wireless telegraphy found applications in maritime communication, enabling ships to send distress signals and messages across vast ocean expanses. The development of vacuum tubes in the 1920s further advanced wireless technology, leading to the emergence of broadcast radio, which brought news, entertainment, and music to households worldwide. The 1930s witnessed the birth of television broadcasting, allowing people to see and hear events as they happened, revolutionizing the way information and entertainment were delivered. World War II played a pivotal role in the evolution of wireless technology, with innovations such as radar systems and secure military communication systems, which were instrumental in the outcome of the war. After the war, the proliferation of television broadcasting continued, and radio waves became the primary medium for mass communication and entertainment, fostering cultural exchanges and shared experiences. The late 20th century brought the advent of the cellular phone, a revolutionary development that allowed people to communicate wirelessly while on the move. The first generation of cellular networks, known as 1G, introduced analog voice communication but had limitations in terms of data transmission and coverage. With the launch of 2G networks in the 1990s, digital communication emerged, enabling not only voice calls but also text messaging and basic data services. The introduction of the Short Message Service (SMS) marked a significant shift in how people communicated, making it possible to send written messages quickly and conveniently. The 2G era also witnessed the birth of mobile internet services, albeit at a rudimentary level, paving the way for the data-driven world we live in today. The third generation of wireless networks, or 3G, emerged in the early 2000s, bringing with it faster data speeds, video calling, and the foundation for mobile internet browsing. The 3G era was a turning point, as it laid the groundwork for smartphones and the mobile apps ecosystem that has since become an integral part of our daily lives. In the late 2000s, 4G networks arrived, offering significantly faster data rates and enabling high-quality video streaming, mobile gaming, and a wide range of innovative applications. The rapid adoption of 4G technology revolutionized industries, from entertainment and social media to healthcare and transportation, as it facilitated seamless connectivity and data access. As we entered the 21st century, the demand for wireless data skyrocketed, leading to the development of 5G networks, the fifth generation of wireless technology. 5G promises to deliver unprecedented data speeds, extremely low latency, and massive connectivity, opening up possibilities for autonomous vehicles, augmented reality, and the Internet of Things (IoT). The historical evolution of wireless technology not only transformed the way we communicate but also reshaped entire industries and our daily lives. Beyond communication, wireless technology has found applications in fields as diverse as healthcare, agriculture, and environmental monitoring, enabling remote sensing and data collection on an unprecedented scale. Wireless sensors and IoT devices are now deployed in smart cities, smart homes, and industrial settings, creating interconnected ecosystems that enhance efficiency and sustainability. In the realm of healthcare, wireless technology has enabled telemedicine, wearable health devices, and remote patient monitoring, improving access to healthcare services and patient outcomes. Agriculture has also benefited from wireless technology, with precision agriculture techniques that use wireless sensors and data analytics to optimize crop yields and resource usage. Environmental monitoring systems rely on wireless networks to collect data on air quality, climate, and natural disasters, helping us better understand and respond to environmental challenges. Wireless technology has not only connected people and devices but has also bridged the digital divide, bringing internet access to remote and underserved regions through satellite and wireless broadband technologies. The journey through the historical evolution of wireless technology highlights the remarkable progress we've made in a relatively short period. From the early days of wireless telegraphy to the era of 5G and beyond, wireless communication has evolved into an essential part of our interconnected world, shaping the way we live, work, and communicate. As we continue to push the boundaries of what wireless technology can achieve, the future promises even more remarkable innovations, connecting us in ways we can only imagine. This ongoing journey is a testament to human ingenuity, creativity, and the enduring quest to overcome barriers and connect with one another in ever more profound ways.

Chapter 2: Understanding Wireless Network Architecture

To delve into the world of wireless networks, it's essential to understand the key components that make them function seamlessly. At the heart of any wireless network is the wireless router, a device that serves as the central hub for data transmission. The wireless router connects to the internet and manages the flow of data between devices within your network and the wider internet. One of the router's core functions is to provide a Wi-Fi signal that allows wireless devices, such as smartphones, laptops, and smart home devices, to connect wirelessly to the network. Inside the wireless router, you'll find several critical components, including the central processing unit (CPU), memory, and storage. These components work together to execute routing functions, handle network traffic, and store configuration settings. The router's firmware, a type of software embedded in the device, plays a pivotal role in ensuring its proper operation. It governs everything from network security to Quality of Service (QoS) settings, allowing you to customize and optimize your network. To communicate wirelessly with the router, each device must be equipped with a network interface card (NIC) or a wireless adapter. These components enable devices to send and receive data through radio waves, forming a wireless connection with the router. Within the router and your connected devices, Wi-Fi antennas play a critical role in transmitting and receiving data over the airwaves. The number and type of antennas can vary, with some routers equipped with multiple external antennas for improved signal strength and coverage. In addition to the router, another essential component is the modem, which bridges the gap between your local network and the internet service provider (ISP). The modem modulates and demodulates signals to convert data between the digital format used by your devices and the analog signals used by your ISP's network. In many cases, you'll find a combination device called a modem-router or gateway, which integrates both modem and router functions into a single device. These devices simplify the setup process and are commonly provided by ISPs to their subscribers. In a wireless network, each device has a unique identifier called a Media Access Control (MAC) address. The MAC address is a hardware-based address that helps the router and other devices on the network identify each other. It plays a crucial role in routing data to the correct destination and enabling secure communication between devices. To ensure the security of your wireless network, encryption is employed to protect the data transmitted between devices and the router. One common encryption protocol used in Wi-Fi networks is Wi-Fi Protected Access (WPA), with versions like WPA2 and WPA3 providing varying levels of security. WPA encrypts the data using a secret passphrase or pre-shared key (PSK), preventing unauthorized access to your network. As part of network security, the router employs a firewall, which acts as a barrier between your local network and the broader internet. The firewall filters incoming and outgoing traffic, allowing legitimate data to pass while blocking potential threats and unauthorized access attempts. Access control lists (ACLs) and port forwarding rules are often used to define the specific traffic that is permitted or denied by the firewall. For remote access to your network, Virtual Private Network (VPN) support may be integrated into the router. VPNs create encrypted tunnels that allow secure communication over public networks, ensuring the privacy and security of your data. Quality of Service (QoS) settings within the router enable you to prioritize certain types of network traffic. This is particularly useful for ensuring a smooth online experience, as you can prioritize activities like online gaming or video streaming. Network management features in the router's firmware provide tools for configuring and monitoring the network. You can use these features to set up guest networks, update firmware, view connected devices, and monitor network performance. In a wireless network, the signal strength and coverage area are critical factors in providing a reliable connection. Factors like the router's transmit power, antenna design, and interference from other electronic devices can influence signal quality. Range extenders or mesh Wi-Fi systems can be used to expand the coverage area of your network, ensuring a strong signal throughout your home or office. Now that we've explored the fundamental components of a wireless network, you have a solid foundation for understanding how these elements work together to create a seamless and secure wireless experience. Wireless network topologies are the architectural designs that define how devices are interconnected within a wireless network. One of the most common types of wireless network topologies is the point-to-point topology. In a point-to-point network, two devices are directly connected wirelessly, forming a one-to-one relationship. Point-to-point connections are often used for tasks like linking two buildings in a campus or establishing a dedicated link between a router and a satellite receiver. Moving beyond point-to-point, we encounter the point-to-multipoint topology, also known as a star topology. In a point-to-multipoint network, a single central device, such as a wireless access point (AP) or router, connects to multiple client devices. This design is typical in home Wi-Fi networks, where a wireless router serves as the central hub, linking laptops, smartphones, and other devices. Another common wireless network topology is the mesh topology. In a mesh network, every device can communicate directly with every other device, creating a highly interconnected and redundant network. Mesh networks are known for their reliability, as they can self-heal by finding alternative paths if one device or connection fails. These networks are used in scenarios like smart home automation and large-scale outdoor wireless deployments. An ad-hoc network is a unique topology where devices communicate directly with each other, forming a decentralized and self-organizing network. Ad-hoc networks are often used in situations where infrastructure-based networks (like those using access points) are impractical. For instance, devices in a disaster-stricken area might form an ad-hoc network to enable communication without relying on existing infrastructure. A hybrid network combines different wireless topologies to meet specific requirements. For example, a hybrid network might consist of a wired backbone network connected to multiple wireless access points, forming a combination of bus and star topologies. Each type of wireless network topology has its advantages and limitations. Point-to-point connections are straightforward and ideal for dedicated links but may not scale well for larger networks. Point-to-multipoint star topologies are easy to manage and suitable for small to medium-sized deployments but can become a single point of failure if the central device fails. Mesh networks offer high reliability but can be complex to configure and manage. Ad-hoc networks are flexible but may have limitations in terms of scalability and performance. Hybrid networks provide a tailored solution by combining different topologies but require careful planning and integration. When designing a wireless network, it's essential to consider factors like coverage area, scalability, reliability, and the specific needs of the devices and applications that will be using the network. By selecting the right wireless network topology, you can create a network that meets your requirements and ensures seamless communication among devices.

Chapter 3: Wireless Encryption and Authentication

Let's embark on a journey into the intriguing world of encryption algorithms and protocols, where digital secrets are shielded and sensitive information remains secure. At its core, encryption is the process of converting readable data, known as plaintext, into an unreadable form, referred to as ciphertext. This transformation is achieved through the use of mathematical algorithms and keys, making it nearly impossible for unauthorized parties to decipher the original data without the proper decryption key. Encryption serves as the foundation of data security in the digital age, safeguarding everything from online banking transactions to confidential email communications. To understand encryption fully, we need to explore the two fundamental components of the process: encryption algorithms and encryption protocols. Encryption algorithms are mathematical formulas designed to perform the encryption and decryption of data. They determine how the plaintext is transformed into ciphertext and how the ciphertext is transformed back into plaintext with the correct decryption key. One of the most widely used encryption algorithms is the Advanced Encryption Standard (AES), which has become the gold standard for securing data. AES operates on blocks of data and supports key lengths of 128, 192, or 256 bits, offering a high level of security. Another well-known encryption algorithm is RSA (Rivest-Shamir-Adleman), which is asymmetric in nature, using a pair of public and private keys for encryption and decryption. RSA is often employed in securing communications and digital signatures. In addition to AES and RSA, there are numerous encryption algorithms with various levels of security and suitability for specific applications. While encryption algorithms provide the mathematical foundation for data security, encryption protocols define how encryption is implemented in practical communication scenarios. One of the most widely used encryption protocols for securing internet communications is Transport Layer Security (TLS). TLS ensures the confidentiality and integrity of data exchanged between web browsers and servers, commonly recognized by the padlock icon in web browser address bars. TLS employs a combination of encryption algorithms, including RSA and AES, to secure data during transit. Another encryption protocol you might encounter is IPsec (Internet Protocol Security), which is used to protect data at the network level. IPsec encrypts and authenticates network packets, ensuring secure communication between devices over IP networks. Beyond these well-known encryption protocols, there are many others tailored to specific use cases, such as securing email (S/MIME), virtual private networks (VPN), and wireless networks (WPA3). Encryption algorithms and protocols work in tandem to provide a layered defense against unauthorized access to data. They ensure that data remains confidential, meaning only authorized parties can access and read it, and that data integrity is preserved, preventing unauthorized tampering or alterations. Additionally, encryption can provide authentication, verifying the identity of the parties involved in a communication. One important aspect to consider when implementing encryption is key management. Encryption keys are the secret ingredients that enable the transformation of plaintext into ciphertext and back. Efficient and secure key management is crucial to maintaining the confidentiality and integrity of encrypted data. Keys can be categorized as symmetric keys, where the same key is used for both encryption and decryption, or asymmetric keys, which use a pair of public and private keys. Symmetric encryption is faster and well-suited for encrypting large volumes of data, while asymmetric encryption excels in scenarios requiring secure key exchange and digital signatures. Key management involves generating, storing, distributing, and securely disposing of encryption keys. It also encompasses key rotation and the establishment of key hierarchies for different levels of access. Effective key management is essential for maintaining the security of encrypted data over time. When implementing encryption in practice, it's important to consider the specific requirements of your application or use case. This includes factors such as the sensitivity of the data, the desired level of security, performance considerations, and compatibility with existing systems and protocols. For example, an e-commerce website that handles sensitive payment information must prioritize strong encryption to protect customer data. On the other hand, a public Wi-Fi network may use encryption to secure user credentials and web traffic while offering convenience and ease of access. It's also essential to stay up-to-date with developments in encryption technology and security best practices. As computing power advances, older encryption algorithms may become vulnerable to attacks, necessitating the transition to more robust encryption methods. Similarly, understanding and adhering to industry standards and regulations related to data security is crucial for ensuring compliance and avoiding legal issues. Encryption is a powerful tool for protecting digital information, and its proper use can mitigate the risk of data breaches and unauthorized access. However, it's important to strike a balance between security and usability, as overly complex encryption schemes can hinder user experience and adoption. In today's interconnected world, where data is constantly in transit and at rest, encryption algorithms and protocols provide a vital layer of defense, ensuring that sensitive information remains confidential and secure.

Let's delve into the fascinating realm of authentication methods in wireless networks, where security and trust play pivotal roles in ensuring that only authorized devices gain access. Authentication is the process of verifying the identity of a device or user before allowing access to a network or system. In wireless networks, this is particularly crucial because they are inherently susceptible to unauthorized access due to their broadcast nature. Without robust authentication measures, anyone within the range of a wireless network could potentially connect to it, potentially compromising its security. One common method of authentication in wireless networks is the use of pre-shared keys (PSKs). With PSK authentication, a network administrator configures a shared passphrase or key that both the access point (AP) or router and the connecting devices must possess. When a device attempts to connect to the network, it must provide the correct passphrase to gain access. PSKs are simple to implement and offer a basic level of security but may have limitations, such as the need to distribute the passphrase to authorized users securely. Another widely used authentication method is the Extensible Authentication Protocol (EAP). EAP is an authentication framework that supports various authentication methods within the framework, making it highly versatile. One popular EAP method used in wireless networks is EAP-PEAP (Protected EAP). EAP-PEAP combines a secure TLS tunnel with username and password authentication, enhancing security by protecting user credentials from eavesdropping. EAP-TTLS (Tunneled Transport Layer Security) is another EAP method that creates a secure tunnel for authentication, making it suitable for protecting user credentials. For enterprises and organizations, the use of EAP methods is often preferable as they offer more advanced security features. A notable EAP method is EAP-TLS (Transport Layer Security), which uses digital certificates for device authentication, providing a high level of security. Certificate-based authentication, such as EAP-TLS, is common in corporate Wi-Fi networks, where strong security is a priority. In addition to PSKs and EAP methods, there's another authentication approach known as MAC address filtering. With MAC address filtering, the wireless router or access point maintains a list of MAC addresses (unique hardware addresses) of authorized devices. Only devices with MAC addresses on this list are granted access to the network. While MAC address filtering is straightforward to set up, it has limitations, including the possibility of MAC address spoofing, where an attacker mimics an authorized device's MAC address to gain access. Furthermore, managing a large number of MAC addresses can become cumbersome. WPA3 (Wi-Fi Protected Access 3) is a newer Wi-Fi security standard that enhances authentication and encryption in wireless networks. It introduces Simultaneous Authentication of Equals (SAE), also known as Dragonfly, as its default authentication method. SAE is a secure key exchange protocol that strengthens the security of the initial connection setup between a device and the wireless router. It protects against common attacks, such as dictionary attacks on PSKs, by making it computationally infeasible for attackers to determine the pre-shared key. As we explore authentication methods in wireless networks, it's important to understand the trade-offs between security and usability. While strong authentication methods like EAP-TLS and WPA3 offer robust security, they may require additional infrastructure and complexity in their implementation. On the other hand, simpler methods like PSKs and MAC address filtering are easier to set up but may not provide the same level of protection against advanced attacks. Security considerations must align with the specific needs and use cases of the wireless network. For example, a home Wi-Fi network may prioritize ease of use and opt for a PSK, while an enterprise network may implement certificate-based authentication for higher security. Multi-factor authentication (MFA) is another authentication strategy gaining prominence in wireless networks. MFA combines two or more authentication factors, such as something you know (password or PIN), something you have (a physical token or smartphone app), and something you are (biometric data like fingerprints or facial recognition). Implementing MFA adds an extra layer of security by requiring users to provide multiple forms of authentication before granting access. This approach significantly reduces the risk of unauthorized access, as even if one authentication factor is compromised, others remain intact. When selecting an authentication method for a wireless network, it's essential to consider factors like the network's size, the sensitivity of the data being accessed, and the resources available for implementation and maintenance. Strong authentication measures are particularly critical for protecting sensitive information and ensuring the integrity of the network. In the ever-evolving landscape of wireless network security, staying informed about the latest authentication methods and best practices is essential for maintaining a secure and reliable network. Wireless networks continue to play a pivotal role in our connected world, and robust authentication methods are the foundation upon which their security rests. As we navigate the complexities of authentication in wireless networks, let's remember that striking the right balance between security and usability is key to creating a network that is both secure and user-friendly.

Chapter 4: Securing Your Wi-Fi Router

Navigating the intricacies of router security settings is akin to fortifying the gateway to your digital realm, ensuring that your network remains resilient against potential threats and intrusions. Routers, the central hubs of our home and office networks, are the guardians that stand between the wilds of the internet and the sanctuary of our digital lives. To bolster this defense, it's imperative to comprehend and configure router security settings effectively. One of the foundational elements of router security is the management interface, where all configurations and settings reside. By default, most routers are accessible via a web-based graphical user interface (GUI) or a command-line interface (CLI). This interface allows you to configure various aspects of the router, such as network settings, security parameters, and access controls. To shield this interface from unauthorized access, it's essential to change the default login credentials. The default usernames and passwords for routers are often well-known and published online, making them vulnerable to exploitation by malicious actors. Changing the login credentials to unique, strong values is the first line of defense against unauthorized access to your router. Another critical aspect of router security is firmware updates. Router manufacturers periodically release firmware updates that patch vulnerabilities, improve performance, and enhance security. Staying vigilant and ensuring that your router's firmware is up-to-date is paramount in maintaining a secure network. Router manufacturers often provide an automated update feature that simplifies the process of keeping the firmware current. Additionally, it's advisable to regularly check the manufacturer's website for firmware updates, as not all routers support automatic updates. While updating firmware is essential, it's equally important to back up your router's settings before making any changes. Router settings can be intricate, and a simple mistake or a firmware update gone awry can lead to a malfunctioning router. Creating a backup of your router's configuration ensures that you can easily restore it to a working state in case of any issues. Most routers include an option to export the configuration to a file that you can save to a secure location. Now, let's delve into wireless security, a crucial component of router settings. Wireless networks are vulnerable to eavesdropping and unauthorized access, making it essential to secure them effectively. The first step in wireless security is to change the default Wi-Fi network name (SSID) and password. Using default values makes it easier for attackers to identify and target your network. Select a unique SSID that doesn't reveal personal information and set a strong Wi-Fi password. When configuring the Wi-Fi password, aim for a combination of upper and lower-case letters, numbers, and special characters, making it difficult to guess. To add an additional layer of security, consider implementing WPA3 (Wi-Fi Protected Access 3) encryption, the latest Wi-Fi security standard. WPA3 offers enhanced security features compared to its predecessor, WPA2, protecting your wireless traffic from eavesdropping and brute-force attacks. Many routers support both WPA2 and WPA3, so ensure that you select the most secure option available. Guest networks are another valuable feature that enhances router security settings. These isolated networks allow visitors to connect to the internet without gaining access to your primary network. Enabling a guest network prevents guests from accessing your sensitive files, devices, and settings. Additionally, you can often set usage limits and restrictions for guest networks to ensure they don't consume excessive bandwidth. Access control is a potent tool for router security. It allows you to specify which devices are allowed or denied access to your network based on their MAC (Media Access Control) addresses. This feature can be used to create whitelists, which only permit known, authorized devices to connect. Conversely, you can create blacklists to block specific devices or prevent unwanted guests from accessing your network. Beyond MAC address filtering, many routers support IP address-based access control, which allows you to control access based on IP addresses. Access control provides an additional layer of defense, especially when dealing with devices that may not support strong authentication methods. Firewalls are another essential component of router security settings. They act as a barrier between your internal network and the untrusted internet. Most routers have built-in firewalls that you can configure to filter incoming and outgoing traffic. You can define rules that specify which types of traffic are allowed or blocked based on source and destination IP addresses, ports, and protocols. Firewalls also provide protection against common attack vectors, such as port scanning and Distributed Denial of Service (DDoS) attacks. To maximize the effectiveness of your firewall, regularly review and update the rules to adapt to changing threats and security requirements. Virtual Private Networks (VPNs) have gained popularity as a means to enhance online privacy and security. Some routers offer built-in VPN support, allowing you to create a secure tunnel for all your internet traffic. This can be particularly valuable when accessing sensitive information or using public Wi-Fi networks. Implementing a VPN at the router level ensures that all devices connected to your network benefit from the added layer of encryption and anonymity. Router security settings extend to Quality of Service (QoS) controls, which allow you to prioritize specific types of network traffic. QoS settings ensure that critical applications, such as online gaming or video conferencing, receive the necessary bandwidth and low latency for optimal performance. By giving priority to essential traffic, you can prevent network congestion from affecting critical activities. Finally, router security settings encompass remote management controls. Some routers allow you to manage the device remotely, which can be convenient for troubleshooting and configuration. However, enabling remote management introduces security risks, as it provides an additional attack vector for malicious actors. If you require remote access, consider restricting it to specific IP addresses and use strong authentication methods like secure VPN connections. In summary, router security settings play a pivotal role in safeguarding your network and digital assets. By diligently configuring and maintaining these settings, you can create a robust defense against potential threats and ensure the privacy and security of your online activities. Whether you're protecting your home network or managing the security of a corporate infrastructure, understanding and implementing router security settings is a fundamental step toward a safer digital world.

Configuring firewall and access controls is akin to setting up digital gatekeepers for your network, ensuring that only the right traffic flows in and out. Firewalls, in essence, act as the sentinels of your network, carefully inspecting every packet of data that attempts to cross their path. They evaluate these packets against a set of predefined rules and policies, determining whether they should be allowed or denied entry. Firewalls come in two primary flavors: hardware and software. Hardware firewalls are dedicated devices designed to protect a network, often found in corporate environments. Software firewalls, on the other hand, are applications that run on individual devices, such as computers or smartphones, providing protection at the device level. A typical home network setup involves a hardware firewall embedded in the router, complemented by software firewalls on individual devices. To configure a firewall effectively, you must first define the rules governing the traffic it will permit or block. Firewall rules are created based on various criteria, including source and destination IP addresses, ports, and protocols. These criteria help the firewall make informed decisions about which packets to allow and which to drop. When crafting firewall rules, it's important to strike a balance between security and functionality. Overly restrictive rules may block legitimate traffic, causing inconvenience and connectivity issues. Conversely, lax rules may expose your network to potential threats and attacks. Firewalls typically include default rules to allow essential traffic like web browsing and email, but it's advisable to customize these rules to suit your specific needs. For instance, if you're running a web server on your network, you'll need to create rules to permit incoming traffic on the web server's port. Network Address Translation (NAT) is a fundamental aspect of many firewall configurations. NAT allows multiple devices on a local network to share a single public IP address when connecting to the internet. It acts as a translator, modifying the source IP address of outgoing packets to the router's public IP address and vice versa for incoming packets. NAT is critical for conserving public IP addresses and protecting internal network structures from external threats. Access controls complement firewall rules by allowing or denying access to specific resources based on user credentials. These controls are commonly used in conjunction with firewalls to enforce security policies. Access control mechanisms often include username and password authentication, ensuring that only authorized users can access sensitive resources. Two-factor authentication (2FA) is an enhanced access control method that adds an extra layer of security by requiring users to provide two forms of verification before granting access. Typically, this involves something the user knows (like a password) and something the user has (like a one-time code from a mobile app). Access controls also extend to role-based access control (RBAC), a method of managing user privileges based on predefined roles within an organization. RBAC allows administrators to assign specific permissions to users or groups, streamlining access management and minimizing security risks. Access control lists (ACLs) are a common tool for specifying what resources a user or group can access. ACLs define permissions and restrictions at a granular level, specifying which users or groups can perform specific actions on resources. For instance, an ACL can specify that only administrators have permission to modify system settings, while regular users can only view them. In addition to ACLs, role-based access control is used to simplify user management by grouping users into roles with similar access requirements. By assigning roles to users, administrators can efficiently manage permissions for large numbers of users while maintaining security. Effective firewall and access control configurations require a deep understanding of your network's topology and security requirements. This includes identifying the critical assets that need protection, such as servers, databases, and sensitive data. Once you've identified these assets, you can design firewall rules and access controls to safeguard them. It's essential to regularly review and update firewall rules and access controls to adapt to changing security threats and network requirements. Regular audits and assessments help ensure that your firewall and access control configurations remain effective in protecting your network. Another essential aspect of firewall and access control management is intrusion detection and prevention systems (IDPS). IDPS tools continuously monitor network traffic for suspicious or unauthorized activity and can automatically respond to detected threats. When configured to work in tandem with firewalls and access controls, IDPS tools provide an additional layer of security by identifying and mitigating threats in real time. Effective firewall and access control configurations are an integral part of network security, helping organizations safeguard their digital assets and maintain data integrity. By carefully crafting firewall rules, implementing access controls, and staying vigilant about security threats, you can create a robust defense against unauthorized access and cyberattacks. As you embark on the journey of configuring firewall and access controls, remember that security is an ongoing process, requiring constant vigilance and adaptation to evolving threats. By approaching these tasks with a proactive mindset and staying informed about the latest security best practices, you can bolster the security of your network and protect your digital assets effectively.

Chapter 5: Basic Security Best Practices

Let's embark on a journey into the realm of strong passwords and user authentication, where the keys to digital security are crafted and wielded to safeguard our online identities and data. In today's interconnected world, where we rely on numerous online services and platforms, strong passwords are the first line of defense against unauthorized access. A strong password is more than just a combination of characters; it's a shield that protects your digital presence from malicious actors. Creating a strong password begins with complexity – the more complex, the better. A strong password typically includes a mix of upper and lower-case letters, numbers, and special characters. Avoid using easily guessable information like common words, phrases, or patterns. Instead, opt for a combination that appears random and is challenging to decipher. Length is another crucial aspect of a strong password. The longer your password, the harder it becomes for attackers to crack it through brute force. Aim for a minimum of 12 characters, and consider even longer passwords for added security. Avoid using personal information like birthdays, names of family members, or easily discoverable details as part of your password. Such information can be readily exploited by attackers who may have access to your public profiles or social media accounts. Creating unique passwords for each of your online accounts is essential. Reusing passwords across multiple accounts is a security risk, as a breach on one platform could compromise all your accounts. Consider using a password manager to generate, store, and autofill complex passwords for different services. Password managers offer the convenience of not having to remember multiple passwords while enhancing security. Regularly updating your passwords is a good practice to mitigate the risk of unauthorized access. Even strong passwords can become vulnerable if they are not changed periodically. Set a schedule to update your passwords and ensure that you're not using the same password for an extended period. Two-factor authentication (2FA) is a powerful tool that enhances user authentication by requiring two forms of verification before granting access. The first factor is typically something you know, like a password, while the second factor is something you have, like a one-time code from an authentication app. Enabling 2FA provides an additional layer of security, making it much more challenging for attackers to gain access, even if they have your password. Many online services, from email providers to social media platforms, offer 2FA options that you can enable in your account settings. Biometric authentication methods, such as fingerprint recognition and facial recognition, have become increasingly prevalent in recent years. These methods leverage unique physical characteristics to verify a user's identity, adding an extra layer of security. Biometric authentication is often used in smartphones and other devices to unlock them securely. While biometric authentication is convenient and secure, it's essential to protect your biometric data and ensure that it is not compromised. Security questions, also known as challenge questions, are a common form of authentication used to verify a user's identity. These questions typically require answers that only the user would know, such as the name of their first pet or the city where they were born. It's crucial to select security questions with answers that are not easily discoverable or guessable by others. Avoid using information that can be found on social media profiles or public records. Single Sign-On (SSO) is a user authentication process that allows users to access multiple applications or services with a single set of login credentials. SSO simplifies the user experience, as users don't need to remember separate passwords for each service. However, it's essential to ensure that the SSO provider has robust security measures in place to protect your login credentials. When using SSO, it's crucial to maintain the security of the primary account, as compromising it could grant access to all linked services. Multi-factor authentication (MFA) is an advanced authentication method that combines two or more authentication factors to verify a user's identity. MFA can include something you know (password), something you have (a smartphone or authentication token), and something you are (biometric data). This approach significantly reduces the risk of unauthorized access, as an attacker would need to compromise multiple factors to gain entry. Some services and organizations require employees or users to undergo periodic security training to raise awareness about best practices in password security and user authentication. Security training can help individuals recognize phishing attempts, password reuse risks, and the importance of strong authentication. It's also essential to educate users about the consequences of sharing passwords or leaving them in easily accessible locations. User authentication is a cornerstone of digital security, protecting sensitive information and personal data. Implementing strong passwords and authentication methods is essential for safeguarding your online presence and ensuring that only authorized individuals can access your accounts and data. By following best practices in password creation and authentication, you can build a robust defense against cyber threats and protect your digital identity in an increasingly connected world. Remember, the keys to a secure online life are in your hands, and with the right practices, you can wield them effectively to keep your digital castle safe from intruders. Let's dive into the realm of regular software updates and patching, where the digital landscape is fortified against vulnerabilities, ensuring the integrity and security of our digital ecosystems. In today's fast-paced and interconnected world, software has become an integral part of our daily lives, powering everything from our smartphones to our computers, and even our household appliances. With this ubiquitous presence comes an inevitable reality - the presence of vulnerabilities and weaknesses in software. No software is immune to these vulnerabilities, as they can be inadvertently introduced during development or discovered later by cybercriminals. These vulnerabilities create potential entry points for attackers, who exploit them to compromise systems, steal data, or disrupt operations. The process of software updates and patching is the means by which these vulnerabilities are identified, addressed, and remedied. It is a crucial component of cybersecurity, acting as a shield against a barrage of evolving threats in the digital landscape. Software updates, also known as patches or fixes, are released by software vendors to address identified vulnerabilities and improve the overall functionality and performance of their products. These updates can take the form of security patches, bug fixes, feature enhancements, or compatibility improvements. One of the most critical reasons for regular software updates is the mitigation of security vulnerabilities. As vulnerabilities are discovered, software vendors work diligently to create patches that close these security holes. By applying these updates, users can protect their systems from potential exploitation by attackers who seek to exploit these weaknesses. Patching is not limited to operating systems; it extends to applications, firmware, and other software components. Applications, including web browsers, office suites, and productivity tools, are commonly targeted by cybercriminals. Therefore, keeping all software, not just your operating system, up to date is essential for maintaining a secure digital environment. Firmware updates, often associated with hardware devices like routers, cameras, and smart home gadgets, play a significant role in cybersecurity. Firmware is the software embedded in hardware devices, and vulnerabilities in firmware can have serious consequences. Firmware updates can address security flaws, enhance device performance, and add new features. Many devices now support automatic firmware updates, ensuring that the latest security fixes are applied without user intervention. However, it's important to regularly check for firmware updates for devices that do not support automatic updates. One of the primary reasons some users hesitate to apply software updates promptly is the fear of compatibility issues or system instability. While it's true that occasionally, an update can introduce new problems, the overall benefits of patching far outweigh the risks. Most software vendors rigorously test updates before release to minimize such issues. In the rare event that an update does cause problems, vendors typically release follow-up patches to address them quickly. Another reason for updating software is the inclusion of new features and enhancements. While security is paramount, software updates often bring valuable improvements to the user experience, adding functionality, streamlining operations, and enhancing performance. For instance, updates to web browsers may introduce faster rendering engines or improved privacy features, making your online experience smoother and more secure. Keeping software up to date is not just an individual responsibility; it is a collective effort. Organizations, from small businesses to large enterprises, must prioritize software patching as a fundamental aspect of their cybersecurity strategy. Unpatched software is one of the primary vectors that cybercriminals target to gain unauthorized access to corporate networks and sensitive data. Therefore, organizations should establish patch management policies and procedures to ensure that software updates are applied promptly and consistently across their systems. Automated patch management solutions can streamline the process, making it easier to deploy updates across a network efficiently. Furthermore, organizations should conduct risk assessments to prioritize which systems and software components require immediate patching. This approach helps allocate resources effectively and ensure that critical vulnerabilities are addressed promptly. In addition to mitigating vulnerabilities and improving functionality, regular software updates contribute to compliance with industry standards and regulations. Many sectors, such as finance, healthcare, and government, have specific cybersecurity requirements that organizations must meet. Failing to keep software up to date can result in non-compliance and potential legal consequences. For example, the General Data Protection Regulation (GDPR) in Europe mandates that organizations take measures to protect personal data, which includes applying security patches to prevent data breaches. Third-party software components, libraries, and dependencies used in applications and systems are also susceptible to vulnerabilities. Managing these external dependencies is a crucial part of software development and maintenance. Open-source libraries, which are prevalent in software development, can be sources of vulnerabilities if not monitored and updated regularly. Developers should regularly audit and update dependencies to ensure that their software remains secure and free from known vulnerabilities. While software updates and patching are fundamental to cybersecurity, it's important to consider the human element in the equation. User awareness and education play a vital role in maintaining a secure digital environment. Users should be informed about the importance of software updates and encouraged to apply them promptly. Phishing emails and malicious websites often exploit unpatched vulnerabilities, making user awareness a critical line of defense. In summary, regular software updates and patching are the cornerstones of digital security in our interconnected world. By diligently applying updates to operating systems, applications, firmware, and other software components, users and organizations can protect themselves against known vulnerabilities and reduce the risk of cyberattacks. While concerns about compatibility and stability are valid, the benefits of patching far outweigh the risks, as updates not only enhance security but also improve functionality and performance. In the ongoing battle against cyber threats, staying vigilant and proactive in applying software updates is a crucial step in safeguarding our digital lives and ensuring a safer digital future for all.

Chapter 6: Detecting and Preventing Unauthorized Access

Let's explore the fascinating realm of Intrusion Detection Systems (IDS), the vigilant guardians of our digital domains, tirelessly monitoring network traffic and system activities to uncover signs of unauthorized access or malicious behavior. In today's interconnected world, where the flow of data is constant and dynamic, the need for robust security measures is paramount. While firewalls and antivirus software provide essential protection, IDS serves as an additional layer of defense, focusing on the detection of anomalous or suspicious activities. The primary function of an IDS is to identify potential security incidents by scrutinizing network traffic, system logs, and other data sources for patterns indicative of cyberattacks or unauthorized access attempts. IDS operates in real-time, continuously analyzing incoming and outgoing data, making it a critical component of any comprehensive cybersecurity strategy. There are two primary categories of IDS: network-based and host-based. Network-based IDS (NIDS) monitors network traffic, analyzing data packets to detect irregularities or known attack signatures. NIDS sensors are strategically placed throughout the network, allowing for comprehensive coverage and the ability to identify threats at the network level. Host-based IDS (HIDS), on the other hand, focuses on individual devices or hosts within the network. HIDS software is installed on each host, monitoring activities such as file system changes, log entries, and application behavior. Both NIDS and HIDS have their strengths and are often used together to provide comprehensive intrusion detection capabilities. An essential aspect of IDS is the ability to differentiate between normal and suspicious activities. This is achieved through the use of predefined rules and signatures, which serve as the basis for identifying potential threats. These rules are developed based on known attack patterns and behaviors, allowing the IDS to recognize familiar malicious activities. However, relying solely on predefined rules has limitations, as it may not detect previously unseen or zero-day attacks. To address this challenge, anomaly detection techniques are employed, which establish a baseline of normal behavior and flag deviations from that baseline as potential intrusions. Anomaly detection can identify previously unknown threats, making it a valuable complement to signature-based detection. Intrusion Detection Systems are designed to operate in two main modes: passive and active. In passive mode, the IDS observes and analyzes network traffic or system activities without taking direct action. When suspicious activity is detected, the IDS generates alerts or notifications for security personnel to investigate further. Active mode, on the other hand, allows the IDS to take proactive measures in response to detected threats. These measures may include blocking specific network traffic or isolating compromised hosts to prevent further damage. While active mode can enhance security by mitigating threats in real-time, it also carries the risk of false positives, potentially disrupting legitimate activities. The effectiveness of an IDS relies heavily on the quality and accuracy of its rules and signatures. These rules need to be continually updated to adapt to evolving threats and vulnerabilities. Security researchers and organizations maintain and distribute these rules, ensuring that IDS systems are equipped to detect the latest threats. Many IDS solutions offer the flexibility to customize and fine-tune rules to suit the specific needs of an organization or network. Tailoring rules allows security teams to focus on the most critical threats and reduce false positives. Intrusion Detection Systems are valuable tools for security incident response. When an IDS detects suspicious activity or a potential intrusion, it generates alerts that are sent to security personnel for investigation. These alerts provide valuable information, including details about the detected activity, the source IP address, and the nature of the potential threat. Security analysts can use this information to assess the severity of the alert, identify the affected systems, and take appropriate actions to mitigate the threat. Effective incident response may involve isolating compromised systems, applying patches, or implementing additional security measures to prevent future attacks. Intrusion Detection Systems can also aid in forensic investigations by providing a record of past security events and activities. This historical data is valuable for analyzing the scope and impact of security incidents, as well as identifying potential weaknesses in the network's defenses. One significant advantage of IDS is its ability to detect a wide range of threats and attacks. These include but are not limited to malware infections, unauthorized access attempts, denial-of-service attacks, and insider threats. By monitoring network traffic and system activities comprehensively, IDS systems can identify both external and internal threats, providing a holistic view of the security landscape. To maximize the effectiveness of an IDS, it is essential to integrate it into a broader security infrastructure. This integration enables the sharing of information and intelligence between different security tools and systems. For example, an IDS can provide data to a Security Information and Event Management (SIEM) system, allowing for centralized log analysis and correlation. By combining information from various sources, security teams can gain a more comprehensive understanding of the threat landscape and respond more effectively to security incidents. Intrusion Detection Systems are not a silver bullet for cybersecurity; they are one piece of the puzzle. A robust security strategy should encompass multiple layers of defense, including firewalls, antivirus software, access controls, and employee training. However, IDS plays a vital role in detecting threats that may otherwise go unnoticed. As cyber threats continue to evolve and become more sophisticated, the importance of IDS in the overall security posture of organizations cannot be overstated. By diligently monitoring network traffic and system activities, IDS systems help protect against a wide range of threats, providing valuable insights and early warning capabilities. Intrusion Detection Systems are the silent sentinels of our digital world, tirelessly standing guard to protect our data, systems, and networks from those who seek to exploit vulnerabilities and compromise our security. In a constantly evolving threat landscape, the role of IDS remains indispensable, serving as a vigilant guardian of our digital realm.

Let's delve into the intriguing world of access control measures and policies, where the keys to digital fortresses are distributed judiciously to safeguard sensitive data, systems, and resources from unauthorized access. In today's interconnected and data-driven landscape, controlling who can access what, when, and how is fundamental to maintaining security and privacy. Access control serves as the digital gatekeeper, determining who is granted entry into the realm of digital assets and who is kept at bay. At its core, access control is about striking a balance between enabling authorized users to access the resources they need while preventing unauthorized users from breaching security. Access control measures encompass a wide array of techniques, policies, and technologies that collectively form the foundation of a robust cybersecurity posture. Authentication, the process of verifying the identity of a user, is the first line of defense in access control. Effective authentication ensures that users are who they claim to be before granting them access. Common authentication methods include passwords, biometrics (such as fingerprints or facial recognition), smart cards, and token-based systems. The choice of authentication method depends on the sensitivity of the resources being protected and the risk tolerance of the organization. Passwords, though widely used, can be susceptible to breaches if not managed properly. Strong password policies, which mandate complex, frequently changed passwords, help mitigate this risk. Biometrics provide a high level of security but may require specialized hardware and raise privacy concerns. Smart cards and tokens are physical devices that users must possess to gain access, adding an additional layer of security. Once a user's identity is verified, authorization determines what actions or resources that user is allowed to access. Authorization is based on a user's role, job responsibilities, or specific permissions assigned within the system. Role-based access control (RBAC) and attribute-based access control (ABAC) are commonly used authorization models. RBAC assigns users to roles, with each role having specific permissions associated with it. ABAC, on the other hand, takes into account various attributes of the user, resource, and environment to make access decisions. Both models can be effective, depending on the organization's needs and the complexity of the access control requirements. Access control lists (ACLs) and policy-based access control (PBAC) are mechanisms that facilitate authorization by specifying which users or groups can access specific resources. ACLs define access permissions at a granular level, listing the users or groups allowed or denied access to a particular resource. PBAC relies on policies that define access rules and conditions, providing more flexibility in access control. Effective access control also includes monitoring and auditing user activities to detect and respond to suspicious or unauthorized actions. Security Information and Event Management (SIEM) systems play a crucial role in this aspect by collecting and analyzing log data from various sources to identify anomalies. Regularly reviewing audit logs and conducting security assessments are essential to ensure that access control policies are effective and enforced. Access control policies are the written guidelines that specify how access control measures should be implemented within an organization. These policies outline the rules, procedures, and best practices that govern who has access to what resources and under what circumstances. Access control policies are not one-size-fits-all; they should be tailored to the unique needs and risk profile of each organization. A critical aspect of access control policies is the principle of least privilege (POLP), which advocates granting users the minimum level of access required to perform their job functions. By adhering to POLP, organizations can minimize the risk of unauthorized access and limit the potential damage that can result from security breaches. Role-based access control aligns closely with the principle of least privilege, as users are assigned roles that correspond to their job responsibilities and access needs. In addition to POLP, the separation of duties (SoD) principle is another important concept in access control. SoD aims to prevent conflicts of interest and fraud by ensuring that no single user has complete control over critical processes or systems. For example, in financial systems, SoD may require that the person who approves payments is different from the person who initiates them. The implementation of access control measures and policies extends beyond the digital realm to include physical security. Physical access control measures, such as access cards, biometric scanners, and security guards, ensure that only authorized personnel can enter secure areas like data centers or server rooms. Combining physical and logical access control enhances overall security by creating a multi-layered defense. Mobile device management (MDM) and bring-your-own-device (BYOD) policies are increasingly critical components of access control. As more employees use personal devices for work-related tasks, organizations must establish policies and controls to manage and secure these devices. MDM solutions enable organizations to enforce security policies, remotely wipe devices, and protect corporate data on mobile devices. BYOD policies outline the rules and expectations for employees who use their personal devices for work, ensuring a balance between convenience and security. Access control policies should be living documents that evolve with the organization's changing needs and the evolving threat landscape. Regular reviews and updates to access control policies are essential to adapt to new technologies, emerging threats, and regulatory changes. Failure to maintain and enforce access control measures and policies can result in security breaches, data loss, and compliance violations. Access control is a cornerstone of cybersecurity, safeguarding sensitive data, protecting critical systems, and ensuring the privacy of individuals. By implementing robust authentication and authorization mechanisms, establishing access control policies, and regularly auditing and updating access controls, organizations can create a secure digital environment that empowers authorized users while thwarting potential threats. Access control is the key to unlocking a world where security and convenience coexist harmoniously, where the right people access the right resources, and where the digital fortress stands strong against intruders.

Chapter 7: Protecting Personal Devices in a Wireless Network

Let's explore the intricate world of device-level security settings, where the guardians of our digital gadgets stand vigilant, ready to protect our devices from a multitude of threats and vulnerabilities. In our modern era, where digital devices are ubiquitous, the need for robust security measures has never been greater. Device-level security settings encompass a wide array of configurations and options that empower users to fortify the defenses of their smartphones, tablets, laptops, and other digital companions. The security of these devices is of paramount importance, as they store sensitive information, connect to networks, and perform a myriad of tasks critical to our personal and professional lives. One of the foundational pillars of device-level security settings is the authentication process, which ensures that only authorized users can access the device. Common authentication methods include PINs, passwords, biometrics (such as fingerprints or facial recognition), and pattern locks. These methods provide the initial layer of defense against unauthorized access. Users are encouraged to choose strong, complex passcodes and enable biometric authentication when available, as these measures significantly enhance device security. Screen lock timeout settings further bolster device security by automatically locking the device after a period of inactivity, requiring authentication to unlock. This feature prevents unauthorized access in case the device is left unattended. Beyond device access, encryption is a crucial component of device-level security. Encryption protects the data stored on the device by converting it into an unreadable format without the proper decryption key. Modern devices often come with built-in encryption capabilities, which users can activate to safeguard their data. Full-disk encryption ensures that even if the device falls into the wrong hands, the data remains secure and inaccessible without the encryption key. Remote wipe and device tracking features are valuable additions to device-level security settings. In the event that a device is lost or stolen, these features enable users to remotely erase their data and, in some cases, track the device's location. Remote wipe ensures that sensitive information does not fall into the wrong hands, while device tracking aids in recovery efforts. Application permissions are another essential aspect of device security. Modern smartphones and tablets allow users to control which permissions apps can access. For example, users can grant or deny an app access to their location, camera, contacts, and other sensitive data. Reviewing and managing app permissions is crucial to prevent applications from accessing information they don't need and potentially compromising user privacy. Device-level security settings also encompass network-related features that protect against various threats. Firewalls, typically associated with computers, are now available on some mobile devices, allowing users to filter incoming and outgoing network traffic. Firewalls help block malicious network activity and enhance device security. Virtual Private Networks (VPNs) are commonly used to encrypt internet traffic and maintain privacy when using public Wi-Fi networks. By configuring a VPN on their device, users can ensure that their data remains encrypted and secure while browsing the web or accessing online services. Device-level security settings extend to antivirus and anti-malware applications, which are essential for protecting devices from malicious software. Regularly updating and running antivirus scans help identify and remove malware threats that may have infiltrated the device. Device manufacturers and software developers frequently release updates and patches to address security vulnerabilities. Keeping the device's operating system and applications up to date is a crucial aspect of device-level security. These updates often include security patches that address known vulnerabilities, reducing the risk of exploitation by cybercriminals. Users should enable automatic updates whenever possible to ensure that their devices are protected against emerging threats. Access control settings allow users to manage who can access their devices. This feature is particularly important for shared devices or those used by multiple family members. By setting up user accounts and defining access permissions, users can maintain control over who can use the device and what they can access. App stores, such as Apple's App Store and Google Play, offer a curated selection of applications that have undergone security reviews. Downloading apps only from reputable sources reduces the risk of downloading malicious software. Users should exercise caution and avoid sideloading apps from untrusted sources, as they may contain malware. In addition to app stores, parental control settings are valuable for safeguarding devices used by children. These settings allow parents to restrict access to certain apps, websites, and content, ensuring a safer digital experience for young users. Device-level security settings extend to physical security as well. Enabling device tracking and remote wipe features can assist in locating and protecting lost or stolen devices. In addition, users should be mindful of their device's physical security, ensuring that it is not left unattended in public places or exposed to potential theft. Backing up device data regularly is an important precautionary measure. In the event of device loss, theft, or damage, having a recent backup ensures that critical data can be restored on a replacement device. Device-level security settings are not static; they should be continually reviewed and updated to adapt to evolving threats and user needs. Regularly auditing and adjusting these settings is a proactive approach to maintaining device security. Education and awareness play a vital role in device-level security. Users should stay informed about common security threats and best practices. Security awareness helps users recognize phishing attempts, malicious apps, and other potential risks. In summary, device-level security settings are the cornerstone of protecting our digital companions and the valuable information they contain. By configuring authentication methods, enabling encryption, managing app permissions, and staying informed about security best practices, users can fortify the defenses of their devices. In a world where digital threats are ever-present, device-level security settings empower users to take control of their digital safety and ensure that their devices remain trusted companions in an increasingly connected world. Device-level security settings are the digital guardians that stand watch over our devices, preserving our privacy, safeguarding our data, and allowing us to navigate the digital landscape with confidence.

Let's embark on a journey through the realm of endpoint security, where the protection of our devices, from laptops to smartphones and everything in between, is paramount to safeguarding our digital lives in an ever-evolving threat landscape. In today's interconnected world, our endpoints, which encompass all the devices we use daily, serve as gateways to the digital realm. They store our sensitive information, connect us to networks, and enable us to perform a multitude of tasks, both personal and professional. Endpoint security, therefore, is not merely an option; it is an imperative to ensure the confidentiality, integrity, and availability of our data and systems. At the heart of endpoint security best practices is the notion that security should be layered, comprehensive, and proactive. To fortify the defenses of our devices, we must consider a multifaceted approach that encompasses both preventive and detective measures. One of the foundational aspects of endpoint security is robust authentication. Authentication ensures that only authorized users can access a device. It often involves the use of strong, unique passwords or passphrases, biometrics like fingerprints or facial recognition, and multi-factor authentication (MFA). MFA adds an extra layer of security by requiring users to provide multiple forms of verification, such as something they know (password) and something they have (a mobile app or token). It's essential to encourage users to create and maintain strong passwords and enable MFA whenever possible. Another critical facet of endpoint security is the use of encryption. Encryption converts data into a secure, unreadable format that can only be deciphered with the appropriate decryption key. Devices should be configured to encrypt data both at rest (when stored on the device) and in transit (when transmitted over networks). Full-disk encryption, a common practice, ensures that even if a device is lost or stolen, the data remains inaccessible without the encryption key. Software updates and patch management are integral components of endpoint security. Operating systems, applications, and firmware must be regularly updated to address known vulnerabilities and security weaknesses. Security patches, provided by device manufacturers and software developers, help close these vulnerabilities and minimize the risk of exploitation. Users should enable automatic updates whenever possible to ensure that their devices are protected against emerging threats. Regularly reviewing and adjusting app permissions is another crucial aspect of endpoint security. Applications on devices often request access to sensitive data, such as location information, contacts, or camera and microphone usage. Users should carefully consider which permissions to grant and be cautious about apps that request excessive access to data that they don't need. Endpoint security extends beyond individual devices to include network security features. Firewalls, often associated with computers, can now be found on many types of devices, including smartphones and tablets. These firewalls filter incoming and outgoing network traffic, helping to block malicious activity and enhance overall device security. Endpoint detection and response (EDR) solutions provide advanced threat detection and remediation capabilities. These solutions continuously monitor device activities, looking for signs of suspicious or malicious behavior. If such behavior is detected, EDR solutions can take automated actions to contain the threat and prevent further damage. Endpoint security also includes antivirus and anti-malware software. These tools help protect devices from a wide range of threats, including viruses, Trojans, ransomware, and other malicious software. Regularly updating and running antivirus scans is essential to identifying and removing malware threats. Backing up data is a critical preventive measure that should not be overlooked. Regularly backing up data ensures that in the event of device loss, theft, or data corruption, critical information can be restored on a replacement device. Remote wipe and device tracking features are invaluable in the event that a device is lost or stolen. These features enable users to remotely erase their data and, in some cases, track the device's location. Remote wipe ensures that sensitive information does not fall into the wrong hands, while device tracking aids in recovery efforts. Endpoint security also encompasses physical security considerations. Users should be mindful of their devices' physical security, ensuring that they are not left unattended in public places or exposed to potential theft. Lock screens and screen timeout settings help protect devices from unauthorized access when left unattended. Furthermore, configuring strong access control settings, such as passwords and biometric authentication, adds an additional layer of defense against unauthorized access. In organizations, mobile device management (MDM) and endpoint management solutions are crucial for managing and securing devices. These solutions allow IT administrators to enforce security policies, remotely wipe devices, and monitor device activities, ensuring that devices comply with organizational security standards. User education and awareness play a pivotal role in endpoint security. Users should stay informed about common security threats and best practices. Security awareness helps users recognize phishing attempts, malicious apps, and other potential risks, reducing the likelihood of falling victim to attacks. Finally, it's important to acknowledge that endpoint security is an ongoing process. Threats and vulnerabilities continually evolve, requiring a proactive approach to security. Regularly reviewing and adjusting security settings, staying informed about emerging threats, and keeping devices and software up to date are essential practices. In summary, endpoint security is a multifaceted discipline that requires a holistic approach to protect our devices and data. By implementing robust authentication, encryption, software updates, app permissions, and security features, users can fortify the defenses of their endpoints. Moreover, awareness, education, and proactive measures are key elements in the ongoing battle to maintain the security of our digital companions. Endpoint security is not merely a choice; it is a responsibility—one that empowers us to navigate the digital world with confidence, knowing that our devices are fortified against threats and vulnerabilities. Endpoint security is the guardian that watches over our digital companions, ensuring that they remain steadfast protectors of our data, privacy, and digital well-being.

Chapter 8: Guest Network Security

Let's delve into the world of setting up a guest network, where the boundaries between hospitality and security converge, allowing us to provide internet access to our visitors while safeguarding our primary network. In our interconnected world, offering a guest network is a common practice, whether it's in our homes or within a business environment. A guest network allows friends, family, or clients to connect to the internet without gaining access to our main network, which may contain sensitive information and devices. The primary goal of setting up a guest network is to strike a balance between convenience and security. By doing so, we can offer internet access to guests without exposing our primary network to potential threats or unauthorized access. The first step in establishing a guest network is to ensure that your router or network device supports this feature. Most modern routers offer guest network functionality, allowing you to create a separate network for guests. Access to this feature is typically found in the router's web-based administration interface. Once you've confirmed that your router supports guest networks, you can proceed with the setup. Access the router's administration interface through a web browser by entering its IP address, which is often printed on the router itself or provided in the router's documentation. Log in using your router's administrative credentials. Navigate to the section of the router's settings that pertains to guest networks. The exact location and wording may vary depending on your router's make and model, but it's typically labeled as "Guest Network" or something similar. Before enabling the guest network, you'll need to configure its settings. Decide on the network name (SSID) for the guest network. This is the name that guests will see when they search for available Wi-Fi networks. While it can be similar to your primary network name, it's a good practice to differentiate it by appending "Guest" or something similar. Choose a secure and unique password for the guest network. This password should be different from the one used for your primary network. While you want to make it convenient for guests to connect, it should still be reasonably strong to deter unauthorized users. Some routers may allow you to set bandwidth limits for the guest network. This can be useful to prevent guests from consuming excessive bandwidth, ensuring a fair share for everyone on the network. Consider whether you want to enable or disable guest network isolation. Enabling isolation prevents devices on the guest network from communicating with each other. This can enhance security but may limit certain types of connectivity if needed for specific purposes. After configuring these settings, enable the guest network. Once enabled, your router will broadcast both the primary network and the guest network, allowing guests to connect using the provided SSID and password. When guests connect to the guest network, they will have internet access, but they won't be able to access devices or resources on your primary network. This segregation helps protect your main network from potential security risks associated with guest devices. Some routers may offer additional features for guest networks, such as time limits and scheduling. You can set specific times when the guest network is active, ensuring it's only available when needed. You can also configure a time limit for guest network access, which automatically disconnects guests after a set period. These features provide added control and security for your guest network. Regularly review and update your guest network settings. Change the guest network password periodically to enhance security, especially if you've had many different guests over time. Additionally, consider disabling the guest network when it's not in use to further reduce potential risks. Educate your guests about the guest network's purpose and limitations. Make it clear that the guest network is for internet access only and that they should not expect access to devices or resources on your primary network. Provide them with the guest network name (SSID) and password for easy connection. Setting up a guest network is a thoughtful way to provide internet access to your visitors while safeguarding your primary network's security. By configuring the guest network settings, differentiating it from your main network, and periodically updating its password, you can ensure that your guests enjoy a convenient and secure online experience. Moreover, the ability to schedule access times and set time limits adds an extra layer of control and security to your guest network. Educating your guests about the purpose and limitations of the guest network helps manage expectations and ensures a positive experience for everyone. In summary, setting up a guest network is a hospitality gesture that balances convenience and security. By implementing best practices and periodically reviewing and updating your guest network settings, you can provide a secure and enjoyable online experience for your visitors. A well-configured guest network not only offers connectivity but also peace of mind, knowing that your primary network remains protected from potential threats. Setting up a guest network is a way of extending a warm digital welcome to your guests while keeping your digital home secure and private.

Let's explore the concept of isolation and segmentation for guest users, a crucial aspect of network management that ensures a secure and controlled environment for visitors while protecting your primary network. In our interconnected world, providing internet access to guests is a common practice, whether at home or in a business setting. However, it's essential to strike a balance between offering convenience to guests and maintaining the security of your network. This is where isolation and segmentation come into play. Isolation refers to the practice of separating one network from another to prevent them from communicating with each other. In the context of guest users, isolation ensures that devices connected to the guest network cannot access devices or resources on your primary network. This is a fundamental security measure to protect your sensitive information and devices. Segmentation, on the other hand, involves dividing a network into smaller, distinct segments. Each segment can have its own rules and permissions, allowing you to control access and traffic flow more granularly. When it comes to guest users, segmentation helps you manage and monitor their activity separately from your primary network. One common method of isolating and segmenting guest users is by setting up a dedicated guest network. Most modern routers and network devices offer this feature, allowing you to create a separate network for guests. This guest network is entirely isolated from your primary network, ensuring that devices on one network cannot communicate with devices on the other. Creating a dedicated guest network is relatively straightforward. Access your router's web-based administration interface and navigate to the section that pertains to guest networks. Here, you can configure the guest network's settings, such as its name (SSID) and password. Choose a unique SSID for the guest network to differentiate it from your primary network. A good practice is to append "Guest" or something similar to the SSID to make it clear that it's intended for guests. Select a secure and unique password for the guest network. While you want it to be convenient for guests, it's essential to keep it reasonably strong to deter unauthorized access. You may also have the option to set bandwidth limits for the guest network, ensuring that guests do not consume excessive bandwidth. This is particularly useful in situations where you want to provide fair access to multiple users. Additionally, some routers offer the option to enable guest network isolation. When enabled, this feature ensures that devices on the guest network cannot communicate with each other. While it enhances security, it may limit certain types of connectivity if needed for specific purposes. After configuring these settings, enable the guest network. Your router will now broadcast both the primary network and the guest network, allowing guests to connect using the provided SSID and password. When guests connect to the guest network, they will have internet access but will be isolated from your primary network. This isolation is a fundamental security measure to protect your primary network from potential threats or unauthorized access. Isolation and segmentation also extend to the business environment. In businesses, guest users often include clients, partners, or vendors who need temporary access to the company's network. Segmenting the guest network ensures that these external users have access to the internet and specific resources they need without compromising the security of the corporate network. For added control and security, businesses can implement a guest portal. A guest portal is a web-based authentication system that requires users to log in or agree to terms of use before gaining access to the guest network. This allows organizations to track guest usage, collect contact information, and enforce network usage policies. Guest portals are particularly valuable in environments where compliance and regulatory requirements need to be met. Regularly review and update your guest network settings, including the SSID and password. Changing the guest network password periodically enhances security, especially if you've had numerous different guests over time. Consider disabling the guest network when it's not in use to further reduce potential risks. Educate your guests about the guest network's purpose and limitations. Make it clear that the guest network is for internet access only and that they should not expect access to devices or resources on your primary network. Provide them with the guest network name (SSID) and password for easy connection. In summary, isolation and segmentation for guest users are essential practices to ensure both convenience and security. By creating a dedicated guest network with isolation features, you can provide internet access to guests while protecting your primary network. Regularly reviewing and updating your guest network settings, along with educating your guests, helps maintain a secure and enjoyable online experience for everyone. In a world where connectivity is vital, isolation and segmentation provide the digital boundaries that allow us to extend hospitality without compromising security. Isolation and segmentation are the digital guards that protect our primary network, ensuring that our guests can enjoy connectivity without encroaching on our digital territory.

Chapter 9: Wi-Fi Security in Public Places

Let's delve into the world of risks and threats associated with public Wi-Fi, a topic of growing importance in our increasingly connected lives, where the conveniences of wireless internet access in public places come with inherent security concerns. In today's digital age, public Wi-Fi has become ubiquitous, providing internet connectivity in places like coffee shops, airports, hotels, and shopping centers. While public Wi-Fi offers the convenience of staying connected on the go, it also introduces a range of security risks and threats that users should be aware of. One of the primary risks associated with public Wi-Fi is the potential for eavesdropping by malicious actors. When you connect to a public Wi-Fi network, your data, including passwords, emails, and personal information, can be intercepted by cybercriminals using techniques like packet sniffing. This is possible because public Wi-Fi networks are often not encrypted or use weak encryption, making it relatively easy for attackers to intercept and access your data. Another significant risk is the presence of rogue hotspots. These are fake Wi-Fi networks set up by attackers to mimic legitimate public networks. Unsuspecting users may unknowingly connect to these rogue hotspots, allowing the attacker to intercept their data and potentially launch various attacks. Man-in-the-Middle (MitM) attacks are a common threat on public Wi-Fi networks. In these attacks, an attacker intercepts communication between two parties, often without their knowledge, to eavesdrop, modify, or steal data. MitM attacks can target sensitive information, such as login credentials and financial data, putting users at risk of identity theft and financial loss. Another threat on public Wi-Fi networks is the distribution of malware. Attackers can use public Wi-Fi as a platform to deliver malicious software to connected devices. Once malware infects a device, it can steal information, spy on users, or cause various forms of damage. Phishing attacks are also prevalent on public Wi-Fi networks. Attackers can set up fake login pages or emails that mimic legitimate services to trick users into revealing sensitive information, such as usernames and passwords. Public Wi-Fi networks are often unencrypted or use weak encryption, making it easier for attackers to intercept and manipulate traffic to launch phishing attacks. Session hijacking is a risk associated with public Wi-Fi, where attackers can take over an active session between a user and a website or service. This can allow the attacker to impersonate the user and gain unauthorized access to their accounts and data. Public Wi-Fi networks are also susceptible to denial-of-service (DoS) attacks, where an attacker floods the network with traffic to disrupt its normal operation. This can result in slow or unreliable internet connectivity for all users connected to the network. A related threat is the creation of malicious Wi-Fi hotspots that intentionally overload users' devices or drain their battery life. Public Wi-Fi networks may lack proper security measures to protect against these attacks. Data leakage is a risk when using public Wi-Fi, as attackers can use various techniques to access and steal data from connected devices. Even seemingly harmless activities, such as browsing websites or accessing cloud storage, can expose sensitive information if the network is compromised. In some cases, public Wi-Fi providers may engage in data collection practices that raise privacy concerns. These providers may monitor users' online activities, track their location, or gather other information for marketing or advertising purposes. Users should be aware of the privacy policies of public Wi-Fi providers and take steps to protect their personal information. Despite these risks and threats, there are steps that users can take to mitigate the security concerns associated with public Wi-Fi. One of the most effective measures is to use a virtual private network (VPN). A VPN encrypts your internet connection, making it difficult for attackers to intercept your data. By using a reputable VPN service, you can browse the web securely and anonymously, even on public Wi-Fi networks. Ensure that your device's operating system and software are up to date. Updates often include security patches that address vulnerabilities that could be exploited by attackers. Avoid accessing sensitive information or conducting financial transactions on public Wi-Fi networks whenever possible. Instead, use cellular data or a secure VPN connection for such activities. When connecting to public Wi-Fi, verify the network's legitimacy. Ask staff for the correct network name or use a hotspot provided by the venue. Turn off sharing and public file access on your device to prevent unauthorized access to your data. Enable two-factor authentication (2FA) on your accounts to add an extra layer of security. Even if an attacker obtains your password, they won't be able to access your accounts without the second authentication factor. Regularly monitor your accounts for any suspicious activity or unauthorized access. Disconnect from public Wi-Fi networks when you're not actively using them to reduce your exposure to potential threats. In summary, public Wi-Fi offers convenience but comes with a range of security risks and threats that users should be aware of. Eavesdropping, rogue hotspots, MitM attacks, malware distribution, phishing, session hijacking, DoS attacks, and data leakage are all concerns on public Wi-Fi networks. However, by taking proactive measures such as using a VPN, keeping devices and software updated, and practicing good security habits, users can mitigate these risks and enjoy a safer online experience while staying connected on the go. Public Wi-Fi may be convenient, but understanding the potential risks and taking steps to protect yourself is essential to navigate the digital world securely. With the right precautions, you can enjoy the benefits of public Wi-Fi without falling victim to its associated threats and vulnerabilities. Let's delve into the world of using Virtual Private Networks (VPNs) for secure access to public Wi-Fi, a powerful tool to safeguard your online privacy and security while enjoying the convenience of wireless internet in various locations. In today's digitally connected world, public Wi-Fi networks are nearly everywhere, from cafes and airports to hotels and shopping malls. While they provide convenient internet access on the go, these networks also come with inherent security risks that can compromise your personal data and online activities. Using a VPN is a valuable strategy to mitigate these risks and enhance your security when connecting to public Wi-Fi. So, what exactly is a VPN, and how does it work? A VPN, or Virtual Private Network, is a technology that creates a secure, encrypted connection between your device and a remote server operated by the VPN provider. This connection forms a tunnel through which your internet traffic is routed, effectively shielding your online activities from prying eyes, such as hackers, cybercriminals, or even your internet service provider (ISP). To use a VPN for secure public Wi-Fi access, you first need to choose a reputable VPN service. There are numerous VPN providers available, both free and paid, each with its own features and capabilities. It's essential to select a VPN provider that aligns with your specific needs, whether it's enhanced security, high-speed performance, or global server coverage. Once you've chosen a VPN provider, you'll need to sign up for an account and install the VPN software or app on your device. Most VPN providers offer applications for a wide range of devices and operating systems, including Windows, macOS, iOS, Android, and more. After installation, launch the VPN app and log in using the credentials provided during registration. Once logged in, you can connect to a VPN server of your choice. VPN providers typically offer a selection of servers located in various countries and regions, allowing you to choose one that suits your preferences. When you connect to a VPN server, your internet traffic is encrypted and routed through that server, making it appear as if your device is located in the same region as the server. This not only enhances your online privacy but also allows you to access content that may be restricted or geo-blocked in your actual location. Now, let's explore the benefits of using a VPN for secure public Wi-Fi access. One of the most significant advantages is enhanced security. By encrypting your internet connection, a VPN protects your data from eavesdropping and interception on unsecured public Wi-Fi networks. Even if malicious actors attempt to intercept your data, they will only see encrypted gibberish, rendering it useless. A VPN also shields you from various threats, such as man-in-the-middle attacks and packet sniffing, which are common on public Wi-Fi networks. Furthermore, a VPN hides your IP address from websites and online services you access while connected to public Wi-Fi. This anonymizes your online activities, reducing the risk of being tracked or monitored by advertisers, ISPs, or cybercriminals. Another benefit of using a VPN is the ability to bypass network restrictions and censorship. In some locations, public Wi-Fi networks may impose restrictions on certain websites, content, or online services. By connecting to a VPN server in a different region or country, you can circumvent these restrictions and access the internet freely and without limitations. Moreover, a VPN adds an extra layer of security when conducting sensitive tasks on public Wi-Fi, such as online banking or shopping. Your encrypted connection ensures that your login credentials, financial transactions, and personal information remain confidential and protected from potential threats. While using a VPN for secure public Wi-Fi access offers numerous advantages, it's essential to be aware of some considerations and best practices. First, choose a reputable VPN provider that prioritizes your privacy and security. Free VPNs may come with limitations or privacy concerns, so it's often worth investing in a paid service that offers better performance and reliability. Second, ensure that your VPN client is updated regularly to receive security patches and enhancements. Outdated VPN software may expose you to vulnerabilities, so stay vigilant and keep your software up to date. Third, while VPNs enhance your security, they do not make you invulnerable. It's crucial to exercise good cybersecurity hygiene by keeping your devices and applications updated, using strong, unique passwords, and being cautious about suspicious websites and emails. Additionally, avoid downloading apps or software from untrusted sources while connected to public Wi-Fi. Finally, be mindful of your VPN's server location when accessing region-specific services. Connecting to a server in a different country may affect your ability to access local content or services, so choose a server location that aligns with your needs. In summary, using a VPN for secure public Wi-Fi access is a wise and effective strategy to protect your online privacy and security. VPNs encrypt your internet connection, shielding your data from eavesdropping and interception on unsecured networks. They also anonymize your online activities, allowing you to browse the web without being tracked or monitored. Furthermore, VPNs enable you to bypass network restrictions and access region-specific content. However, it's crucial to select a reputable VPN provider, keep your VPN software updated, and practice good cybersecurity habits to maximize the benefits of using a VPN on public Wi-Fi. By taking these precautions, you can enjoy the convenience of public Wi-Fi while maintaining the highest level of security and privacy. In an era where staying connected is essential, a VPN becomes your digital guardian, ensuring that you can browse, work, and communicate securely, even on the most untrusted public Wi-Fi networks.

Chapter 10: Troubleshooting and Common Security Issues

Let's dive into the world of troubleshooting wireless connection problems, a skill that can save you from frustrating connectivity issues and help you get the most out of your wireless network. In today's digitally connected world, a reliable wireless connection is crucial for work, communication, entertainment, and more. However, like any technology, wireless networks can encounter problems that disrupt your online experience. Learning how to troubleshoot these issues is essential for maintaining a stable and consistent wireless connection. The first step in troubleshooting wireless connection problems is to identify the nature of the issue. Is the problem affecting all devices connected to your network, or is it isolated to a single device? Understanding the scope of the problem can help narrow down potential causes and solutions. If the issue is isolated to one device, start by troubleshooting that specific device. Common device-related problems include outdated drivers, misconfigured settings, or hardware issues. Ensure that the device's Wi-Fi adapter drivers are up to date, as outdated drivers can lead to connectivity problems. Check the device's network settings to make sure it's connected to the correct network and that DHCP (Dynamic Host Configuration Protocol) is enabled to obtain an IP address automatically. If the problem persists, consider restarting the device, as a simple reboot can resolve many connectivity issues. If multiple devices are experiencing problems, the issue may be with your wireless router or the network itself. Begin by rebooting your wireless router. Unplug the router's power source, wait a few seconds, and then plug it back in. This can often resolve minor connectivity issues and refresh the router's settings. If rebooting the router doesn't solve the problem, check the physical connections. Ensure that all cables are securely plugged in, and inspect the router for any signs of damage or overheating. If you suspect a hardware issue with the router, you may need to contact your router's manufacturer or consider replacing it. Interference from other electronic devices can also disrupt your wireless connection. Cordless phones, microwave ovens, and other wireless devices operating on the same frequency as your Wi-Fi network can cause interference. To mitigate interference, try relocating your wireless router to a different location away from potential sources of interference. Additionally, ensure that your router is operating on the least congested Wi-Fi channel. Most modern routers have an automatic channel selection feature, but you can also manually select a less crowded channel in the router's settings. Wi-Fi signal strength is another common factor in connectivity problems. If you're experiencing weak or inconsistent signals in certain areas of your home or office, consider using a Wi-Fi signal booster or range extender to extend your network's coverage. These devices can improve signal strength and eliminate dead spots. Security settings on your wireless network can also impact connectivity. Ensure that your Wi-Fi network is using strong encryption, such as WPA3, to protect against unauthorized access. Additionally, verify that you're using a secure Wi-Fi password that is not easily guessable. Weak or compromised security can lead to unauthorized access and network disruptions. If you've recently changed your Wi-Fi password, make sure that all connected devices are updated with the new credentials. Sometimes, wireless connection problems may be caused by issues with your internet service provider (ISP). Check if other online services, such as websites or streaming platforms, are also experiencing connectivity problems. If multiple services are affected, contact your ISP to inquire about potential outages or issues on their end. DNS (Domain Name System) settings can impact your ability to access websites and online services. If you're experiencing difficulty accessing specific websites, consider changing your DNS server settings to use a public DNS service like Google DNS or OpenDNS. This can often resolve DNS-related connectivity issues. Network congestion can also lead to slow or unreliable wireless connections. If many devices are using your network simultaneously, it can strain your network's bandwidth. Consider implementing Quality of Service (QoS) settings on your router to prioritize specific devices or types of traffic, ensuring a smoother online experience for critical tasks. If you've exhausted troubleshooting steps and the problem persists, it may be time to contact your internet service provider or seek assistance from a professional network technician. They can diagnose and resolve more complex network issues that may be beyond the scope of basic troubleshooting. In summary, troubleshooting wireless connection problems is an essential skill in today's digital age. By identifying the nature of the issue, checking device settings, rebooting your router, mitigating interference, ensuring strong security settings, and addressing potential ISP or DNS problems, you can resolve most wireless connectivity issues. Additionally, using Wi-Fi signal boosters or range extenders can improve signal strength and eliminate dead spots in your network. Remember that network troubleshooting is a step-by-step process, and patience is key to finding the root cause of the problem. With the right approach, you can maintain a reliable and stable wireless connection, ensuring that your online activities remain uninterrupted and enjoyable. Troubleshooting wireless connection problems is like solving a puzzle, and with the right pieces in place, you can achieve a seamless and reliable wireless experience, no matter where you are. Let's explore the world of addressing common Wi-Fi security challenges, an essential topic to help you fortify your wireless network and protect your digital world from potential threats and vulnerabilities. In today's interconnected landscape, Wi-Fi networks play a pivotal role in our daily lives, enabling us to stay connected, work remotely, stream content, and much more. However, as our reliance on Wi-Fi continues to grow, so does the importance of addressing the security challenges that come with it. One of the most prevalent Wi-Fi security challenges is weak or compromised passwords. Many users still use easily guessable passwords or never change the default passwords that come with their routers. These practices make it relatively straightforward for attackers to gain unauthorized access to your Wi-Fi network. To address this challenge, it's essential to create strong, unique Wi-Fi passwords that are difficult to guess. A strong password typically includes a combination of upper and lower-case letters, numbers, and special characters. Avoid using easily guessable information like birthdates or common words. Additionally, consider changing your Wi-Fi password periodically to enhance security. Another common security challenge is the lack of encryption on Wi-Fi networks. Encryption is essential to protect your data from eavesdropping and interception by unauthorized individuals. Ensure that your Wi-Fi network uses WPA3 encryption, the most secure encryption standard available. Older encryption standards like WEP and WPA2 are vulnerable to attacks and should be avoided whenever possible. Updating your router's firmware is crucial to address known vulnerabilities and improve its overall security. Router manufacturers release firmware updates that include security patches to protect against emerging threats. Failing to update your router's firmware leaves it vulnerable to exploitation by attackers. Check your router's settings regularly for available updates and apply them promptly. Guest network security is another Wi-Fi challenge that deserves attention. Many Wi-Fi routers offer the option to set up a guest network, which provides internet access to visitors without granting them access to your main network. However, guest networks are sometimes left unsecured or with weak passwords, making them vulnerable to unauthorized access. To address this challenge, always enable security features like WPA3 encryption and use strong passwords for your guest network. Limit the access duration for guests, and consider setting up a separate network entirely to isolate guest traffic. Router security settings are often overlooked, but they play a crucial role in protecting your Wi-Fi network. Ensure that remote management features are disabled on your router to prevent unauthorized access. Change the default router login credentials, as attackers often target routers with default usernames and passwords. Regularly review and update your router's security settings to align with best practices and the latest security standards. Wi-Fi security challenges also extend to device-level security. Outdated devices with unpatched software or firmware can become vulnerable targets for attackers. Regularly update your devices' operating systems and applications to patch known vulnerabilities. Consider enabling automatic updates to ensure that you're always running the latest and most secure software versions. Moreover, some devices may not receive regular updates, making them potential security risks. Evaluate the security of older or unsupported devices and replace them if necessary to maintain a secure network. Device-level security also involves securing your smartphones, tablets, and laptops with strong passcodes or biometric authentication. Enable features like remote wipe or device tracking to protect your data in case of loss or theft. Public Wi-Fi networks present unique security challenges. When connecting to public Wi-Fi, always exercise caution. Avoid connecting to open or unsecured networks, as they leave your data exposed to potential eavesdropping. Use a Virtual Private Network (VPN) to encrypt your internet connection and protect your data while on public Wi-Fi. VPNs create a secure tunnel for your traffic, ensuring that even if the network is compromised, your data remains confidential. Social engineering attacks are a significant Wi-Fi security challenge. Attackers may attempt to trick you into revealing sensitive information, such as Wi-Fi passwords or login credentials. Be cautious when receiving unsolicited emails or phone calls requesting such information. Verify the identity of the requester and avoid sharing sensitive data unless you're certain of its legitimacy. Phishing attacks often target Wi-Fi users, so be vigilant about the websites you visit and the emails you open. Secure your network further by enabling network-level security features. Many routers offer intrusion detection and prevention systems (IDPS) that can identify and block suspicious network traffic. These systems can help safeguard your network from various threats, including malware and unauthorized access attempts. To address the challenge of unauthorized devices connecting to your network, enable MAC address filtering. This feature allows you to specify which devices are allowed to connect to your network based on their unique MAC addresses. While MAC address filtering adds an extra layer of security, keep in mind that determined attackers can still spoof MAC addresses, so it should be used in conjunction with other security measures. Lastly, consider using advanced security tools and services to enhance your Wi-Fi network's protection. Intrusion detection systems, firewalls, and network monitoring solutions can help identify and mitigate security threats in real-time. These tools provide an added layer of defense against unauthorized access and malicious activities. In summary, addressing common Wi-Fi security challenges is crucial in today's digital landscape. Weak passwords, encryption vulnerabilities, guest network security, router settings, device-level security, and the risks associated with public Wi-Fi networks all demand attention to maintain a secure wireless environment. By following best practices such as using strong passwords, enabling WPA3 encryption, updating firmware, securing guest networks, and being cautious on public Wi-Fi, you can fortify your Wi-Fi network's security. Remember that Wi-Fi security is an ongoing process that requires vigilance and regular updates to stay ahead of emerging threats. With the right knowledge and proactive measures, you can enjoy the benefits of Wi-Fi connectivity while safeguarding your digital world from potential vulnerabilities and attacks. Addressing Wi-Fi security challenges is like building a fortress around your digital domain, ensuring that your network remains a safe and secure haven in an increasingly interconnected world.

BOOK 2
HACKING WI-FI NETWORKS
INTERMEDIATE TECHNIQUES FOR PENETRATION TESTERS

ROB BOTWRIGHT

Chapter 1: Intermediate Wi-Fi Security Fundamentals

Let's embark on a journey to explore Wi-Fi encryption protocols, a vital aspect of securing your wireless network and protecting your data from prying eyes in our interconnected world. In the realm of Wi-Fi security, encryption is the cornerstone that shields your data from unauthorized access and eavesdropping. It transforms the information traveling between your devices and your Wi-Fi router into an unreadable format for anyone without the encryption key. Essentially, it's like encoding your data in a secret language that only you and your authorized devices understand. There are several Wi-Fi encryption protocols available, each with its level of security and compatibility. One of the oldest and least secure encryption methods is WEP, or Wired Equivalent Privacy. WEP uses a static encryption key, and its weaknesses have made it obsolete. In fact, it's relatively easy for attackers to crack WEP encryption and gain access to your network. To protect your network, it's essential to avoid using WEP and instead opt for stronger encryption options. WPA, or Wi-Fi Protected Access, was introduced to address WEP's vulnerabilities. WPA uses a more robust encryption method and provides better security for your Wi-Fi network. However, it's still susceptible to certain attacks, particularly if you use a weak passphrase. WPA2, an improved version of WPA, became the standard for Wi-Fi security for many years. It introduced the Advanced Encryption Standard (AES) protocol, which significantly enhanced network security. WPA2 uses a strong encryption key that is much more challenging for attackers to crack than WEP or WPA. For a long time, WPA2 was considered secure enough for most home and business networks. However, as technology advances, so do the tools and methods that attackers use. In recent years, security researchers discovered vulnerabilities in WPA2, known as KRACK (Key Reinstallation Attacks), which raised concerns about its security. As a result, the Wi-Fi Alliance introduced WPA3, the latest and most robust Wi-Fi encryption protocol to date. WPA3 addresses the vulnerabilities of its predecessors and introduces several key security enhancements. One of the notable features of WPA3 is its resistance to offline dictionary attacks, making it much more challenging for attackers to guess your Wi-Fi password. It also provides individualized data encryption, ensuring that even if an attacker compromises one device on the network, they cannot decrypt the data of other devices. Additionally, WPA3 enhances security for open Wi-Fi networks, such as those found in public places, by using Opportunistic Wireless Encryption (OWE). This feature encrypts data transmission even on open networks, significantly improving security for users connecting to public Wi-Fi. WPA3's introduction of a stronger 192-bit security suite provides an extra layer of protection for networks with higher security requirements. It's worth noting that while WPA3 offers substantial improvements in Wi-Fi security, it may not be backward-compatible with older devices that support only WPA or WPA2. For such cases, many routers offer mixed mode, which allows them to support both WPA2 and WPA3 simultaneously. This ensures that older devices can still connect securely while newer ones benefit from the enhanced security of WPA3. Now, let's address the practical steps to ensure your Wi-Fi network is using the most robust encryption protocol available. First, log in to your router's administration interface. You can typically access this by entering the router's IP address into a web browser. Refer to your router's documentation or manufacturer's website for the specific address and login credentials. Once logged in, navigate to the wireless security settings. Here, you'll find options to select the encryption protocol and set a passphrase. Choose WPA3 or WPA2/WPA3 mixed mode as your encryption method. If your router supports WPA3, it's advisable to use it for the highest level of security. Next, create a strong passphrase for your Wi-Fi network. A strong passphrase is typically a combination of upper and lower-case letters, numbers, and special characters. Avoid using easily guessable information, such as common words or phrases. Longer passphrases are generally more secure, so aim for at least 20 characters. Remember to save your passphrase in a secure place, as you'll need it to connect new devices to your network. Finally, apply the changes, and your router will configure the selected encryption protocol. Be aware that all your previously connected devices will need to reconnect using the new passphrase. In summary, Wi-Fi encryption protocols are fundamental to securing your wireless network. Choosing the right encryption protocol, such as WPA3, ensures that your data remains confidential and protected from unauthorized access. Regularly update your router's security settings to stay ahead of emerging threats and vulnerabilities. By following these steps and best practices, you can enjoy a secure and worry-free Wi-Fi experience, knowing that your data is shielded from prying eyes in our interconnected world. Wi-Fi encryption is like a fortress guarding your digital realm, and with the right protocols in place, your data remains safe and secure in an ever-evolving digital landscape. Let's delve into the world of authentication mechanisms in Wi-Fi networks, a critical aspect of network security that ensures only authorized users gain access to your wireless environment. Authentication is the process by which a network verifies the identity of a user or device before granting access. Think of it as a digital bouncer at the door of a nightclub, checking IDs to allow only those on the list to enter. In Wi-Fi networks, various authentication mechanisms are employed to validate the credentials of users and devices. One of the most common authentication methods is the use of pre-shared keys (PSK). This method requires users or devices to enter a passphrase, also known as a Wi-Fi password, to gain access to the network. PSK authentication is straightforward and widely used in home networks, making it convenient for users who have the correct passphrase. However, it has limitations in terms of security, especially if the passphrase is weak or easily guessable. Weak passphrases are susceptible to brute force attacks, where attackers attempt to guess the passphrase through trial and error. To enhance security when using PSK, it's crucial to choose a strong, complex passphrase that includes a mix of upper and lower-case letters, numbers, and special characters. Avoid using easily guessable information like common words or phrases. Another authentication mechanism used in Wi-Fi networks is 802.1X, which is a more robust and versatile method. 802.1X is often used in enterprise or business environments where a higher level of security is required.

It involves the use of a Remote Authentication Dial-In User Service (RADIUS) server, which authenticates users or devices attempting to connect to the network. With 802.1X, each user or device must provide unique credentials, such as a username and password, before being granted access. This ensures that only authorized individuals or devices can connect to the network. 802.1X also supports other authentication methods, such as digital certificates and smart cards, providing additional layers of security. Digital certificates, in particular, are highly secure as they require the possession of a unique certificate to gain access to the network. However, implementing 802.1X authentication can be more complex and may require additional infrastructure, such as a RADIUS server. Once set up, it provides a robust and secure authentication mechanism for Wi-Fi networks. An extension of 802.1X authentication is Wi-Fi Protected Access (WPA) and its successor, WPA2. These Wi-Fi security standards use 802.1X as the authentication framework while also incorporating encryption to secure data transmission. WPA and WPA2 offer a significant security improvement over the earlier WEP (Wired Equivalent Privacy) standard, which was vulnerable to attacks. The use of 802.1X authentication, combined with strong encryption methods like AES (Advanced Encryption Standard), enhances the overall security of Wi-Fi networks. WPA3, the latest iteration of Wi-Fi security, continues to build on these principles, introducing even stronger encryption and security enhancements. Another authentication mechanism used in Wi-Fi networks is MAC address filtering. MAC (Media Access Control) addresses are unique identifiers assigned to network interface cards in devices. With MAC address filtering, network administrators can create a list of approved MAC addresses. Only devices with MAC addresses on this list are allowed to connect to the network. While MAC address filtering provides an additional layer of security, it should not be solely relied upon as a security measure, as determined attackers can spoof MAC addresses. Additionally, managing a large list of MAC addresses can become cumbersome in larger networks. In enterprise environments, Single Sign-On (SSO) authentication is often used to streamline user access. SSO allows users to log in once with a single set of credentials, and those credentials are then used to access multiple services, including Wi-Fi networks. This simplifies the authentication process for users while maintaining security. SSO can be integrated with various authentication protocols, including 802.1X, to ensure secure access to Wi-Fi networks. While these authentication mechanisms are valuable tools for securing Wi-Fi networks, it's essential to consider other security measures in tandem. Strong encryption, regularly updated security settings, and network monitoring are crucial components of a comprehensive security strategy. Additionally, staying informed about emerging security threats and vulnerabilities is essential to maintaining the security of your Wi-Fi network. In summary, authentication mechanisms in Wi-Fi networks play a pivotal role in ensuring that only authorized users and devices gain access to the network. Options such as pre-shared keys, 802.1X, MAC address filtering, and Single Sign-On provide varying levels of security to accommodate different network requirements. Choosing the appropriate authentication method and implementing it effectively is essential for safeguarding your network from unauthorized access and potential security breaches. Remember that security is an ongoing process, and regularly updating your network's security measures is crucial to staying ahead of emerging threats in our ever-evolving digital landscape. Authentication mechanisms in Wi-Fi networks are like the digital gatekeepers, ensuring that only trusted guests gain access to your network's party while keeping uninvited intruders at bay.

Chapter 2: Reconnaissance and Information Gathering

Let's delve into the intriguing world of passive reconnaissance techniques, a fundamental aspect of gathering information about target systems and networks without directly interacting with them. Imagine you're a digital detective, and your mission is to uncover valuable insights about a potential target. In the realm of cybersecurity, passive reconnaissance is your Sherlock Holmes-like investigation, relying on observation and data analysis. It's a subtle approach that leaves no traces, making it an essential skill for ethical hackers, security professionals, and anyone interested in understanding the digital landscape. Passive reconnaissance begins with the collection of publicly available information. This information, often referred to as open-source intelligence (OSINT), can be found through various means, such as online searches, social media, public records, and domain name registrations. Think of it as piecing together a puzzle, with each fragment of information providing a clearer picture of the target. For example, domain name registrations can reveal the names and contact details of individuals or organizations associated with a website. Social media profiles may expose employees' names, roles, and even details about their interests. Public records might disclose business addresses, financial information, or legal disputes related to the target. This initial phase of passive reconnaissance involves collecting breadcrumbs that may lead to more valuable insights. Once you've gathered a substantial amount of publicly available information, it's time to analyze and organize your findings. This phase is akin to arranging puzzle pieces to form a coherent image. You'll want to categorize the information you've collected, creating a structured overview of the target. Consider organizing data by categories such as personnel, infrastructure, technologies, and affiliations. By doing so, you can identify potential vulnerabilities, attack vectors, or areas of interest. While passive reconnaissance primarily focuses on collecting non-intrusive data, it's essential to maintain ethical boundaries. Always respect privacy and adhere to legal and ethical guidelines when gathering information. Your goal is to understand and protect, not to invade or harm. One valuable source of information in passive reconnaissance is the Domain Name System (DNS). DNS translates human-readable domain names into IP addresses that computers use to communicate. When you query a DNS server for a domain name, it often reveals associated IP addresses, subdomains, and sometimes the type of services hosted on those addresses. By examining a target's DNS records, you can uncover valuable insights about its online infrastructure. For instance, subdomains like "mail," "vpn," or "admin" can indicate the existence of specific services or access points. Another technique in passive reconnaissance involves network scanning and enumeration. While this may seem intrusive, in passive reconnaissance, it's done indirectly by observing network traffic without actively probing or interacting with the target. By examining network traffic, you can identify active hosts, services, and protocols in use. For instance, analyzing traffic may reveal that a target organization uses a specific email provider, remote access solutions, or content management systems. This information can be crucial for understanding the target's technology stack and potential vulnerabilities. Passive reconnaissance also extends to email analysis. Publicly available email addresses associated with the target can provide valuable insights. You can use email addresses to identify key personnel, such as IT administrators or executives, who may hold privileged access. Furthermore, analyzing email patterns and domains can help uncover potential third-party services used by the target. Emails often contain footers that disclose software or services in use, which can be valuable for understanding the target's technology landscape. Social media analysis is another facet of passive reconnaissance. People often share information about their professional roles, affiliations, and interests on platforms like LinkedIn, Twitter, or Instagram. By examining the social media profiles of target individuals or organizations, you can gain insights into their activities, connections, and potentially even their technological preferences. Furthermore, online forums and discussion boards can be treasure troves of information. Members of these communities often share their experiences, challenges, and solutions related to technology and security. By lurking in these forums, you can gain knowledge about the target's industry-specific practices, common issues, and potential vulnerabilities. It's essential to maintain a passive presence in such communities, never disclosing your true intentions or attempting to actively engage with members. In passive reconnaissance, you're the silent observer, gathering valuable information while leaving no traces behind. In summary, passive reconnaissance techniques are like the detective work of the digital realm, relying on observation, analysis, and data collection from publicly available sources. By respecting ethical boundaries and adhering to legal guidelines, you can uncover valuable insights about your target's personnel, infrastructure, technologies, and affiliations. Whether you're a cybersecurity professional or a curious enthusiast, passive reconnaissance is a skill worth honing in our ever-evolving digital landscape. It's about understanding and safeguarding, using information as your Sherlockian magnifying glass to uncover hidden clues in the vast expanse of the digital world. Let's venture into the realm of active scanning and network enumeration, an essential part of the reconnaissance phase in cybersecurity. Imagine you're a digital explorer equipped with tools that allow you to map the uncharted territory of computer networks. In the world of cybersecurity, active scanning and network enumeration are your compass and map, helping you navigate and understand the vast digital landscapes. Active scanning involves sending carefully crafted queries or packets to target systems to elicit responses. Think of it as knocking on the doors of networked devices to see who's home and willing to engage in a conversation. The primary purpose of active scanning is to identify active hosts, open ports, and services running on those hosts. It's a bit like exploring a city and determining which buildings are occupied and what businesses operate inside. One of the most commonly used tools for active scanning is Nmap (Network Mapper). Nmap allows you to scan networks and hosts for open ports, services, and operating system information. By sending specific packets to target systems and analyzing the responses, Nmap can provide a detailed view of the network's layout and the services it offers.

Another widely used tool is Wireshark, a packet analysis tool that captures and analyzes network traffic. Wireshark helps you inspect the data exchanged between devices, revealing valuable information about the network's operation and potential vulnerabilities. While active scanning can be a powerful tool for understanding a network, it's essential to use it responsibly and ethically. Unauthorized or aggressive scanning can disrupt network operations and potentially violate legal and ethical boundaries. Before conducting active scans, always seek proper authorization, and ensure that your actions align with legal regulations and ethical guidelines. Now, let's delve into network enumeration, which is the process of gathering detailed information about networked systems and their services. Enumeration is like exploring the interior of a building you've identified during active scanning. You want to learn as much as possible about what's inside and how it operates. Enumeration techniques involve probing target systems to extract information such as user accounts, share names, group memberships, and more. One common enumeration method is SNMP (Simple Network Management Protocol) enumeration. SNMP is a network protocol used for managing and monitoring network devices. It provides a wealth of information about networked systems, including device configurations, performance statistics, and more. Enumeration through SNMP involves querying network devices for data, which can be invaluable for understanding the network's structure and the roles of various devices. Another enumeration technique is DNS enumeration, which involves querying Domain Name System servers for information about hostnames, IP addresses, and other domain-related details. This technique can help map the network's domain structure and identify potential targets for further exploration. LDAP (Lightweight Directory Access Protocol) enumeration is another valuable method for gathering information about users, groups, and organizational units within a network. LDAP is often used for managing user accounts and directory services, making it a prime source of information for attackers or security professionals. During enumeration, you can query LDAP servers to extract user account details, group memberships, and organizational hierarchies. NetBIOS enumeration is particularly useful in Windows environments. NetBIOS is a legacy protocol that provides naming and discovery services in Windows networks. By querying NetBIOS services, you can obtain information about hostnames, share names, and even user account names on networked Windows systems. As with active scanning, it's crucial to approach enumeration responsibly and ethically. Unauthorized or aggressive enumeration can disrupt network operations and compromise security. Always seek proper authorization and follow legal and ethical guidelines when performing network enumeration. To summarize, active scanning and network enumeration are essential techniques for understanding the layout, structure, and operation of computer networks. They provide valuable insights into active hosts, open ports, services, and networked devices. By responsibly applying these techniques, cybersecurity professionals can identify potential vulnerabilities and security weaknesses, ultimately strengthening the network's defenses. However, it's crucial to remember that with great power comes great responsibility, and ethical considerations must guide your actions in the ever-evolving digital landscape. Active scanning and network enumeration are like the explorer's tools in the world of cybersecurity, helping you unveil the hidden treasures and potential pitfalls of networked territories while ensuring you tread responsibly on this digital expedition.

Chapter 3: Advanced Wireless Scanning and Enumeration

Let's embark on a journey into the fascinating world of advanced network mapping and fingerprinting, where you'll discover the techniques and tools used to create detailed maps of computer networks and identify specific devices. Imagine you're an architect tasked with creating a blueprint of a complex and interconnected city, each building representing a networked device. In the realm of cybersecurity, advanced network mapping and fingerprinting are your architectural tools, enabling you to understand the structure, vulnerabilities, and characteristics of a digital landscape. Network mapping is the process of discovering and visualizing the layout of devices and their connections within a network. Think of it as creating a digital map of a sprawling metropolis, highlighting the roads and buildings while providing insights into their functions. Mapping networks is essential for both defensive and offensive cybersecurity efforts, as it helps defenders understand their network's layout and potential weaknesses, while attackers use it to identify targets and potential entry points. One of the primary techniques for network mapping is active scanning, where tools like Nmap are employed to probe target networks. Nmap sends packets to target hosts and analyzes their responses to determine which hosts are online, what services and ports they offer, and sometimes even their operating systems. This information is used to build a comprehensive map of the network, showing which devices are interconnected and how they communicate. Another technique is passive network mapping, which relies on observing network traffic without directly interacting with the target systems. Tools like Wireshark are used to capture and analyze network packets, revealing information about the devices and services in use. By studying traffic patterns and packet data, analysts can create a map of the network's activity and identify key devices. While mapping a network is akin to sketching its layout, fingerprinting takes you a step further by identifying the unique characteristics and attributes of each device. It's like recognizing the architectural style and distinct features of individual buildings in our digital city. Network fingerprinting aims to answer questions like "What specific devices are running on the network?" and "What software versions are they using?" One common fingerprinting technique is banner grabbing, which involves connecting to network services and capturing the banner or banner-like responses they provide. These banners often reveal information about the service, such as its name, version, and sometimes even configuration details. Banner grabbing can be accomplished using tools like Telnet or specialized banner grabbing scripts. Another powerful fingerprinting method is passive OS fingerprinting, which identifies the operating systems running on networked devices without direct interaction. Tools like p0f analyze network packets and extract characteristics that are unique to various operating systems. By comparing these characteristics to a database of known OS signatures, p0f can make educated guesses about the OS running on a target device. The results are often surprisingly accurate, providing valuable insights into the network's diversity of devices and their respective configurations. Another fascinating approach to fingerprinting is fingerprinting web applications and services. This technique focuses on identifying the web applications and technologies used by a target, which can be crucial for understanding potential vulnerabilities. Tools like WhatWeb and Wappalyzer can analyze web responses and HTTP headers to detect web server software, content management systems, programming languages, and more. By fingerprinting web technologies, analysts can uncover potential attack vectors and tailor their strategies accordingly. Network fingerprinting can also extend to protocol-level analysis. For example, identifying the version of a network protocol being used can provide insights into potential vulnerabilities and attack vectors. Analyzing the behavior of the Border Gateway Protocol (BGP) or the Simple Mail Transfer Protocol (SMTP) can help security professionals detect anomalies and potential threats. It's essential to approach network mapping and fingerprinting with care and consideration for ethical and legal boundaries. Unauthorized or aggressive scanning and fingerprinting can disrupt network operations, violate privacy, and potentially lead to legal consequences. Always seek proper authorization and follow ethical guidelines when conducting these activities. In summary, advanced network mapping and fingerprinting are like the artist's tools in the world of cybersecurity, allowing you to create intricate portraits of networked landscapes and recognize the unique characteristics of each device. These techniques are invaluable for both defenders and attackers, providing insights into network layouts, vulnerabilities, and the diversity of devices and technologies in use. However, responsible and ethical conduct is paramount in this digital realm, ensuring that your actions contribute to the security and understanding of our interconnected world. Network mapping and fingerprinting are the brushes and colors that help you paint a detailed and insightful picture of digital networks, making them safer and more secure for all. Let's explore the intriguing world of detecting hidden SSIDs and closed networks, where you'll uncover the techniques and tools used to reveal wireless networks that aren't broadcasting their names. Imagine you're a digital detective, on a mission to unveil hidden secrets in the wireless landscape. In the realm of Wi-Fi security, detecting hidden SSIDs and closed networks is your investigative skill, allowing you to discover networks that prefer to remain incognito. To start, let's clarify what a hidden SSID or closed network is. Most wireless networks broadcast their Service Set Identifier (SSID), which is essentially the network's name. You've likely seen a list of available Wi-Fi networks on your device, each with a recognizable name like "HomeNetwork" or "CoffeeShopGuest." These names are SSIDs, and broadcasting them is the default behavior for most routers. However, some network administrators choose to hide the SSID by disabling broadcast. This makes the network's name invisible to devices actively scanning for available networks. Think of it as a secret club that doesn't advertise its presence. To connect to such a network, you need to know the SSID in advance, as it won't appear in the list of available networks on your device. Now, let's explore how you can detect these hidden SSIDs and closed networks. One common method is passive scanning, where your device listens for "probe requests" from nearby devices. When a device wants to connect to a Wi-Fi network, it sends out probe requests that include the SSID it's looking for. These probe requests are like whispered secrets in the air, and your device can capture them. By analyzing these probe requests, you can discover hidden SSIDs that devices are trying to connect to. Tools like Wireshark can capture and analyze probe requests, revealing hidden network names. Another approach is active scanning, where you send probe requests yourself to elicit responses from hidden networks. This is akin to knocking on the door of the secret club and waiting for a response. Tools like Kismet or Airodump-ng can be used to perform active scans. However, it's important to note that actively scanning for hidden SSIDs may be considered intrusive or even suspicious, depending on the context. Always ensure that your actions are ethical and legal. SSID enumeration is another method used to detect hidden SSIDs. This technique involves sending probe requests with blank or wildcard SSIDs to the network. If the hidden network is configured to respond to such requests, it will reveal its SSID in the response. This is like sending a secret handshake and receiving a friendly reply from the club. Keep in mind that not all hidden networks will respond to blank or wildcard SSIDs, as security measures can vary. Furthermore, some networks may have additional layers of protection, such as MAC address filtering or authentication requirements. Another approach is war-driving or war-walking, where individuals roam around with Wi-Fi scanning equipment to detect hidden networks actively. This is like detectives patrolling the neighborhood, searching for clues. By actively scanning the vicinity, you can discover hidden networks that may not be visible from a fixed location. Once you've detected a hidden SSID, it's important to remember that connecting to it may require knowledge of the network's security credentials, such as the pre-shared key (PSK) or other authentication methods. Furthermore, attempting to connect to a hidden network without authorization is unethical and potentially illegal. Always seek proper authorization and adhere to ethical guidelines when conducting Wi-Fi network discovery. In summary, detecting hidden SSIDs and closed networks is like uncovering hidden gems in the Wi-Fi landscape, using your skills and tools to reveal networks that prefer to remain incognito. Whether you're a network administrator, security professional, or simply curious, understanding these techniques can be valuable in various scenarios. However, ethical conduct and respect for privacy and security are paramount. Remember that the digital realm, like the physical world, has its hidden secrets, and it's up to responsible explorers to unveil them with care and consideration.

Chapter 4: Exploiting Wi-Fi Vulnerabilities

Let's delve into the realm of common Wi-Fi exploitation techniques, where you'll gain insights into the methods attackers use to compromise wireless networks and how to defend against them. Imagine you're the guardian of a digital fortress, responsible for protecting your castle from cunning invaders. In the world of cybersecurity, understanding common Wi-Fi exploitation techniques is your shield, helping you defend against adversaries seeking unauthorized access. Wi-Fi networks have become an integral part of our lives, providing convenient access to the internet and digital services. However, their ubiquity also makes them attractive targets for cybercriminals. To safeguard your network, you must be aware of the tactics they employ. One of the most prevalent Wi-Fi exploitation techniques is the evil twin attack, also known as an access point (AP) spoofing attack. In this scenario, an attacker creates a rogue wireless AP with a name similar to a legitimate network. It's like a wolf in sheep's clothing, luring unsuspecting devices to connect. Once connected, the attacker can intercept traffic, steal sensitive information, or launch further attacks. To defend against evil twin attacks, always verify the legitimacy of Wi-Fi networks, especially in public places, and avoid connecting to open networks without proper authentication. Another common technique is Wi-Fi eavesdropping, where an attacker intercepts and monitors wireless network traffic. Think of it as someone eavesdropping on your conversations in a crowded room. Attackers use tools like Wireshark to capture data packets, potentially revealing sensitive information like login credentials or personal data. To protect against eavesdropping, use encryption protocols like WPA3 and avoid sending sensitive information over unsecured connections. Deauthentication attacks are another concern, where an attacker sends deauthentication packets to disconnect devices from a Wi-Fi network. It's like someone repeatedly slamming the door in your face, preventing you from entering your own home. These attacks can disrupt network access and create opportunities for other exploits. Implementing intrusion detection systems (IDS) can help detect deauthentication attacks and take preventive measures. Man-in-the-middle (MITM) attacks are among the most insidious Wi-Fi exploits. In MITM attacks, the attacker positions themselves between the victim and their intended destination. It's like a surreptitious middleman intercepting and altering your messages. Once in the middle, the attacker can eavesdrop, modify data, or inject malicious code. Using secure protocols like HTTPS and employing certificate validation can mitigate MITM risks. Cracking Wi-Fi passwords is a well-known technique attackers use to gain unauthorized access. By using tools like Aircrack-ng, attackers can attempt to guess or crack Wi-Fi passwords. It's akin to someone trying to pick the lock on your front door. To defend against password cracking, use strong, complex passwords and consider implementing Wi-Fi Protected Access (WPA) security protocols. WPS (Wi-Fi Protected Setup) attacks target vulnerabilities in the WPS feature, which simplifies the process of connecting devices to Wi-Fi networks. Attackers can exploit weak PINs or other flaws to gain access. It's like someone finding a hidden key under your doormat. Disabling WPS on your router can mitigate this risk. Rogue APs are unauthorized access points set up by attackers to trick users into connecting. It's similar to finding a fake ticket booth at an event. Once connected, the attacker can intercept traffic or launch attacks. Regularly scanning for and identifying rogue APs can help maintain network security. SSID (Service Set Identifier) cloaking, also known as hiding the SSID, is a technique used by network administrators to make the network's name invisible to unauthorized users. However, attackers can use SSID enumeration techniques to discover hidden SSIDs. It's like finding a hidden treasure map. Implementing strong encryption and authentication mechanisms can provide an additional layer of security. Evil maid attacks occur when an attacker gains physical access to a device, such as a laptop, that has previously connected to a secure Wi-Fi network. The attacker then installs malicious software, enabling them to intercept network traffic. It's like a crafty hotel maid secretly entering your room. To protect against evil maid attacks, use full-disk encryption and secure boot options. Beacon flooding attacks overload a network with excessive beacon frames, disrupting its normal operation. It's like a relentless car alarm going off in your neighborhood. Intrusion detection systems can help detect and respond to beacon flooding attacks. MAC address spoofing is when an attacker impersonates an authorized device on the network by changing their MAC address. It's akin to someone wearing a disguise to gain access. Using MAC filtering and strong authentication methods can mitigate this risk. Jamming attacks involve flooding the Wi-Fi frequency with noise, disrupting network communication. It's like playing loud music during a conversation. Detecting and locating the source of jamming attacks can be challenging but is crucial for maintaining network availability. To summarize, understanding common Wi-Fi exploitation techniques is essential for protecting your wireless networks from cyber threats. Just as a vigilant guardian watches over a castle, you must safeguard your digital domain. By being aware of these techniques and implementing robust security measures, you can ensure that your Wi-Fi network remains a safe and reliable gateway to the digital world. Remember, in the ever-evolving landscape of cybersecurity, knowledge and vigilance are your greatest allies. With the right defenses in place, you can enjoy the benefits of Wi-Fi connectivity without falling victim to malicious exploits. Let's dive into the intriguing world of leveraging weaknesses in Wi-Fi protocols, where you'll explore the vulnerabilities in the very foundations of wireless communication and how attackers exploit them. Imagine you're an architect inspecting a building's blueprints, searching for hidden flaws that could compromise its structural integrity. In the realm of cybersecurity, understanding weaknesses in Wi-Fi protocols is your blueprint examination, allowing you to identify potential vulnerabilities in wireless communication. Wi-Fi has become an integral part of our lives, enabling us to connect our devices to the internet and each other wirelessly. However, like any technology, Wi-Fi is not immune to weaknesses, and attackers are constantly seeking ways to exploit them. To better understand these vulnerabilities, let's delve into some common weaknesses in Wi-Fi protocols. One of the most well-known weaknesses is the susceptibility of WEP (Wired Equivalent Privacy) encryption. WEP was the original security protocol for Wi-Fi, but it is now considered highly insecure. Attackers can exploit vulnerabilities in the WEP encryption algorithm to intercept and decrypt network traffic. It's like having a lock on your door that can be picked in seconds. To defend against this weakness, it's essential to use stronger encryption methods like WPA3 (Wi-Fi Protected Access 3). Another vulnerability lies in the authentication process of older Wi-Fi protocols. Attackers can perform brute force or dictionary attacks to guess passwords and gain unauthorized access to Wi-Fi networks. It's similar to trying different keys until one unlocks the door. To protect against this weakness, use strong, complex passwords and consider implementing additional security measures like two-factor authentication. An often-overlooked weakness is the lack of protection against rogue access points. Rogue access points are unauthorized devices that mimic legitimate Wi-Fi networks. When devices connect to these rogue APs, attackers can intercept their traffic or launch attacks. It's like having an imposter doorman who lets anyone into your building. Implementing wireless intrusion detection systems (WIDS) can help detect and mitigate rogue APs. Another weakness arises from the inherent nature of Wi-Fi signals, which can extend beyond the intended coverage area. Attackers can use directional antennas and high-power transmitters to eavesdrop on Wi-Fi traffic from a considerable distance. It's akin to listening in on a conversation from a neighboring building. To defend against this weakness, employ physical security measures and encryption to protect data in transit. A significant vulnerability lies in the design of open Wi-Fi networks, which do not require authentication to connect. Attackers can easily intercept traffic on open networks, as it's like having a public conversation anyone can overhear. To protect against this weakness, avoid connecting to open Wi-Fi networks for sensitive activities and use a VPN (Virtual Private Network) for added security. The security of Wi-Fi Protected Setup (WPS) is also a subject of concern. WPS was designed to simplify the process of connecting devices to Wi-Fi networks but has known vulnerabilities. Attackers can exploit weak WPS PINs to gain unauthorized access. It's like having a master key that's easy to replicate. Disabling WPS on your router can mitigate this weakness. Frame replay attacks are another issue, where attackers capture data frames from a legitimate user and replay them to gain access to the network. It's like someone copying your voice to unlock a voice-activated security system. Using protocols with built-in protections against frame replay attacks, like WPA3, can help defend against this weakness. The KRACK (Key Reinstallation Attack) vulnerability shook the Wi-Fi security landscape. KRACK attacks target the WPA2 protocol and exploit weaknesses in the four-way handshake, allowing attackers to intercept and manipulate data. It's like tampering with the secret handshake to gain entry. To defend against this weakness, ensure your Wi-Fi devices are updated with security patches. Another significant vulnerability is the lack of client device security. If a device connecting to a Wi-Fi network is compromised, it can introduce threats to the entire network. It's like having one infected person in a crowded room. Implementing network access controls and regularly updating client devices can mitigate this risk. The use of weak encryption ciphers is another weakness that attackers can exploit. Some Wi-Fi devices and routers may use outdated or vulnerable encryption ciphers, making them susceptible to attacks. It's like using an outdated lock that's easily picked. To defend against this weakness, keep your devices and routers updated with the latest firmware and security patches. Now, let's consider the vulnerability of Wi-Fi Direct, a technology that allows devices to connect directly without the need for a traditional Wi-Fi network. Attackers can exploit weak or nonexistent security measures in Wi-Fi Direct to intercept and manipulate data between devices. It's like having a secret conversation in a crowded room. To protect against this weakness, be cautious when using Wi-Fi Direct and consider using additional security layers. In summary, understanding the weaknesses in Wi-Fi protocols is like examining the structural integrity of a building; it helps you identify potential vulnerabilities and reinforce your defenses. As technology evolves, so do the methods attackers use to exploit these weaknesses. Therefore, it's crucial to stay informed about emerging threats and continuously update your Wi-Fi security measures. By addressing these vulnerabilities, you can enjoy the convenience of wireless connectivity while keeping your digital domain secure. In the ever-changing landscape of Wi-Fi security, knowledge is your strongest asset, allowing you to stay one step ahead of potential attackers. Remember that just as architects design buildings to withstand various challenges, you can fortify your Wi-Fi network against potential threats with the right knowledge and precautions.

Chapter 5: Cracking Wi-Fi Passwords and Keys

Let's embark on a journey into the intriguing world of brute-force and dictionary attacks, where you'll unravel the tactics that attackers employ to crack passwords and gain unauthorized access to systems. Imagine you're a cryptographer deciphering a complex code, where each attempt brings you closer to unveiling the secret within. In the realm of cybersecurity, understanding brute-force and dictionary attacks is like holding the key to recognizing potential threats and fortifying your defenses. Passwords have long been the gatekeepers to our digital world, providing a layer of security for our accounts and data. However, these digital keys are only as strong as their complexity and the methods used to protect them. Brute-force and dictionary attacks are two techniques attackers use to bypass these defenses. Let's delve into these methods and how they work. Brute-force attacks are the digital equivalent of trying every possible combination to unlock a door. Attackers systematically try every possible password until they find the correct one. It's like someone attempting to open a combination lock by trying every combination, starting from 0000 and counting upwards. This method is incredibly time-consuming, but it's effective if the password is weak or simple. To defend against brute-force attacks, it's crucial to use strong, complex passwords. Long passwords with a combination of letters, numbers, and special characters are much more resistant to this type of attack. Additionally, implementing account lockout policies, which temporarily lock an account after a certain number of failed login attempts, can deter brute-force attackers. Dictionary attacks, on the other hand, are more refined and targeted. Instead of trying every possible combination, attackers use a precompiled list of commonly used passwords, known as a dictionary. It's like having a keyring with a list of commonly used keys, trying each one until the right key unlocks the door. Attackers often use dictionaries that include common words, phrases, and known passwords, as well as variations like "password123" or "letmein." To defend against dictionary attacks, it's essential to avoid using easily guessable passwords. Passwords like "123456" or "password" are among the first to be tried in a dictionary attack. Instead, create unique passwords that are not easily found in common dictionaries. Consider using passphrases, which are longer and more secure combinations of words, or use a password manager to generate and store complex passwords. Rainbow tables are another tool that attackers may use in their quest to crack passwords. A rainbow table is a precomputed list of password hashes and their corresponding plaintext passwords. Instead of trying every possible password, attackers can simply look up the hash in the table to find the corresponding password. It's like having a magic decoder that instantly reveals the secret code. To defend against rainbow table attacks, it's crucial to use strong password hashing algorithms, such as bcrypt or scrypt. These algorithms make it much more time-consuming and computationally expensive for attackers to generate rainbow tables. Salting is an additional measure to protect against rainbow table attacks. A salt is a random value added to the password before hashing, ensuring that even identical passwords result in different hashes. Think of it as adding a unique ingredient to each dish you cook, making them distinct. This makes rainbow tables ineffective, as they would need to include every possible salt value. Password policies play a crucial role in defending against brute-force and dictionary attacks. Organizations should implement policies that enforce strong password requirements, such as minimum length, complexity, and regular password changes. It's like setting rules for constructing locks, ensuring they meet certain security standards. Two-factor authentication (2FA) adds an extra layer of protection against these attacks. Even if an attacker obtains the correct password, they would still need the second authentication factor, such as a one-time code sent to a mobile device. It's like requiring both a key and a fingerprint to unlock a secure vault. This significantly enhances security and reduces the effectiveness of brute-force and dictionary attacks. Rate limiting and account lockout policies are valuable defenses. Rate limiting restricts the number of login attempts a user can make within a certain time frame. Account lockout temporarily disables an account after a specified number of failed login attempts. These measures make it difficult for attackers to perform mass brute-force or dictionary attacks. It's like having a bouncer at the door who limits the number of people attempting to enter the club. Intrusion detection systems (IDS) and intrusion prevention systems (IPS) can also be employed to detect and block suspicious login attempts. These systems monitor network traffic and can identify patterns indicative of brute-force or dictionary attacks. It's like having security cameras that alert you when someone is trying to pick a lock. Educating users about password security is essential. Users should be aware of the importance of strong, unique passwords and the risks associated with using weak or common passwords. Training can help them recognize phishing attempts and other social engineering tactics used by attackers. It's like teaching people how to recognize counterfeit currency. In summary, understanding brute-force and dictionary attacks is like knowing the techniques burglars use to break into homes. By recognizing the vulnerabilities in passwords and implementing robust defenses, you can better protect your digital assets. Remember that strong, complex passwords, along with additional security measures like 2FA and account lockout policies, are your first line of defense. Just as a well-fortified fortress is difficult to breach, a well-protected password can deter even the most determined attackers. Stay vigilant, stay informed, and stay secure in the digital realm.

Let's delve into the intriguing world of Wi-Fi WPS (Wi-Fi Protected Setup) vulnerabilities and attacks, where you'll discover the potential security risks associated with this convenience feature and how attackers exploit them. Imagine you're navigating a maze with hidden traps, and WPS vulnerabilities are the pitfalls that attackers seek to exploit. In the realm of cybersecurity, understanding Wi-Fi WPS vulnerabilities and attacks is like having a map to avoid those traps and protect your network. Wi-Fi WPS was introduced as a convenient way to simplify the process of connecting devices to Wi-Fi networks. It was designed to make the setup process quicker and more user-friendly, especially for users who might find traditional Wi-Fi network configuration challenging. However, this convenience comes at a cost – WPS can introduce security vulnerabilities that attackers can exploit. To grasp the significance of WPS vulnerabilities and attacks, let's delve into how WPS works and the associated risks. Wi-Fi Protected Setup (WPS) is a feature that allows users to connect devices to a Wi-Fi network by pressing a physical button on the router or entering a PIN code. The idea is to simplify the process and eliminate the need to manually enter a long, complex Wi-Fi password. It's like having a magic wand that instantly connects your devices to the network without any hassle. WPS offers three primary methods for connecting devices: the Push Button method, the PIN method, and the Near Field Communication (NFC) method. While these methods enhance user convenience, they can also introduce security risks. Let's examine each of these methods and the associated vulnerabilities. The Push Button method is the most straightforward. It involves pressing a physical button on the router and then initiating the connection on the device. Think of it as a handshake that establishes trust between the router and the device. However, this method can be vulnerable to attacks if an attacker gains physical access to the router or is within range to press the button during the setup process. It's like someone sneaking into your home and joining a private gathering. To mitigate this risk, it's essential to physically secure your router in a location inaccessible to unauthorized individuals. The PIN method allows users to connect devices by entering an eight-digit PIN code provided by the router. It's like sharing a secret code to gain access to a secure area. However, the problem with this method is that the PIN is often pre-generated and hardcoded into the router, making it susceptible to brute-force attacks. Attackers can repeatedly guess the PIN until they find the correct combination. It's like trying every possible four-digit code to unlock a phone. To defend against PIN brute-force attacks, it's crucial to disable WPS or change the default PIN to a custom, unique one. The Near Field Communication (NFC) method is a relatively secure way to establish a connection between devices. Users can tap their NFC-enabled device against the router to initiate the connection. It's like sharing digital business cards by tapping phones together. However, this method requires physical proximity, limiting its usefulness for remote attackers. Nonetheless, it's essential to ensure that only authorized devices have physical access to the router. Now, let's explore some of the common vulnerabilities and attacks associated with WPS. One significant vulnerability is the use of default PINs. Many routers come with predefined, hardcoded PINs that attackers can easily discover through online databases or by using tools designed to exploit this weakness. It's like having a master key that can open many doors. To protect against this vulnerability, always change the default PIN to a custom one that is not easily guessable. Another vulnerability arises from the way some routers implement the WPS protocol. Some routers don't implement any rate limiting or lockout mechanisms for failed PIN attempts, making them susceptible to brute-force attacks. It's like having a door that doesn't lock after multiple failed attempts to open it. To defend against this vulnerability, consider using a router that implements rate limiting or lockout policies for WPS attempts. The Pixie Dust attack is a specific type of WPS attack that targets vulnerable routers. It exploits weaknesses in the WPS protocol to reveal the router's WPA/WPA2 encryption key. It's like finding the hidden answer to a riddle. To defend against the Pixie Dust attack, it's essential to disable WPS on your router if you don't use it regularly. In recent years, the Reaver tool has gained notoriety as a popular tool for conducting WPS attacks. It automates the process of guessing WPS PINs and can quickly crack vulnerable routers. It's like having a digital locksmith who can pick locks with ease. Defending against Reaver attacks involves disabling WPS on your router, using strong encryption protocols, and regularly updating your router's firmware to patch known vulnerabilities. In summary, understanding Wi-Fi WPS vulnerabilities and attacks is like being aware of potential hazards in a digital landscape. While WPS was designed to simplify the process of connecting devices to Wi-Fi networks, it can introduce security risks if not properly configured and secured. To protect your network, it's crucial to disable WPS if you don't use it, change default PINs to custom ones, and implement strong encryption protocols. Just as you would secure your home against potential intruders, safeguarding your Wi-Fi network from WPS vulnerabilities and attacks ensures that your digital domain remains safe and secure. Stay vigilant, stay informed, and stay one step ahead of potential attackers.

Chapter 6: Evasion Techniques and Stealthy Attacks

Let's delve into the intriguing world of Wi-Fi WPS (Wi-Fi Protected Setup) vulnerabilities and attacks, where you'll discover the potential security risks associated with this convenience feature and how attackers exploit them. Imagine you're navigating a maze with hidden traps, and WPS vulnerabilities are the pitfalls that attackers seek to exploit. In the realm of cybersecurity, understanding Wi-Fi WPS vulnerabilities and attacks is like having a map to avoid those traps and protect your network. Wi-Fi WPS was introduced as a convenient way to simplify the process of connecting devices to Wi-Fi networks. It was designed to make the setup process quicker and more user-friendly, especially for users who might find traditional Wi-Fi network configuration challenging. However, this convenience comes at a cost – WPS can introduce security vulnerabilities that attackers can exploit. To grasp the significance of WPS vulnerabilities and attacks, let's delve into how WPS works and the associated risks. Wi-Fi Protected Setup (WPS) is a feature that allows users to connect devices to a Wi-Fi network by pressing a physical button on the router or entering a PIN code. The idea is to simplify the process and eliminate the need to manually enter a long, complex Wi-Fi password. It's like having a magic wand that instantly connects your devices to the network without any hassle. WPS offers three primary methods for connecting devices: the Push Button method, the PIN method, and the Near Field Communication (NFC) method. While these methods enhance user convenience, they can also introduce security risks. Let's examine each of these methods and the associated vulnerabilities. The Push Button method is the most straightforward. It involves pressing a physical button on the router and then initiating the connection on the device. Think of it as a handshake that establishes trust between the router and the device. However, this method can be vulnerable to attacks if an attacker gains physical access to the router or is within range to press the button during the setup process. It's like someone sneaking into your home and joining a private gathering. To mitigate this risk, it's essential to physically secure your router in a location inaccessible to unauthorized individuals. The PIN method allows users to connect devices by entering an eight-digit PIN code provided by the router. It's like sharing a secret code to gain access to a secure area. However, the problem with this method is that the PIN is often pre-generated and hardcoded into the router, making it susceptible to brute-force attacks. Attackers can repeatedly guess the PIN until they find the correct combination. It's like trying every possible four-digit code to unlock a phone. To defend against PIN brute-force attacks, it's crucial to disable WPS or change the default PIN to a custom, unique one. The Near Field Communication (NFC) method is a relatively secure way to establish a connection between devices. Users can tap their NFC-enabled device against the router to initiate the connection. It's like sharing digital business cards by tapping phones together. However, this method requires physical proximity, limiting its usefulness for remote attackers. Nonetheless, it's essential to ensure that only authorized devices have physical access to the router. Now, let's explore some of the common vulnerabilities and attacks associated with WPS. One significant vulnerability is the use of default PINs. Many routers come with predefined, hardcoded PINs that attackers can easily discover through online databases or by using tools designed to exploit this weakness. It's like having a master key that can open many doors. To protect against this vulnerability, always change the default PIN to a custom one that is not easily guessable. Another vulnerability arises from the way some routers implement the WPS protocol. Some routers don't implement any rate limiting or lockout mechanisms for failed PIN attempts, making them susceptible to brute-force attacks. It's like having a door that doesn't lock after multiple failed attempts to open it. To defend against this vulnerability, consider using a router that implements rate limiting or lockout policies for WPS attempts. The Pixie Dust attack is a specific type of WPS attack that targets vulnerable routers. It exploits weaknesses in the WPS protocol to reveal the router's WPA/WPA2 encryption key. It's like finding the hidden answer to a riddle. To defend against the Pixie Dust attack, it's essential to disable WPS on your router if you don't use it regularly. In recent years, the Reaver tool has gained notoriety as a popular tool for conducting WPS attacks. It automates the process of guessing WPS PINs and can quickly crack vulnerable routers. It's like having a digital locksmith who can pick locks with ease. Defending against Reaver attacks involves disabling WPS on your router, using strong encryption protocols, and regularly updating your router's firmware to patch known vulnerabilities. In summary, understanding Wi-Fi WPS vulnerabilities and attacks is like being aware of potential hazards in a digital landscape.

While WPS was designed to simplify the process of connecting devices to Wi-Fi networks, it can introduce security risks if not properly configured and secured. To protect your network, it's crucial to disable WPS if you don't use it, change default PINs to custom ones, and implement strong encryption protocols. Just as you would secure your home against potential intruders, safeguarding your Wi-Fi network from WPS vulnerabilities and attacks ensures that your digital domain remains safe and secure. Stay vigilant, stay informed, and stay one step ahead of potential attackers. Let's dive into the intriguing world of evading intrusion detection systems (IDS), where you'll explore the tactics attackers use to bypass these security measures and how to fortify your defenses. Imagine you're playing a game of cat and mouse, where the cat represents the IDS, and the mouse is the clever attacker. In the realm of cybersecurity, understanding evasion techniques is like being the wily mouse, knowing how to navigate the maze without getting caught. Intrusion detection systems are crucial components of network security, designed to monitor and analyze network traffic to identify suspicious or malicious activity. They act as digital sentinels, constantly on the lookout for signs of unauthorized access or unusual behavior. However, just as clever mice find ways to evade the cat's grasp, attackers develop strategies to bypass IDS and infiltrate networks. To grasp the significance of evading IDS, let's delve into how these systems work and the techniques attackers use to circumvent them. Intrusion detection systems come in two primary forms: network-based and host-based. Network-based IDS monitor network traffic and analyze packets to detect suspicious patterns or signatures. It's like having a security camera that scans the environment for unusual movements or behaviors. Host-based IDS, on the other hand, focus on individual devices or hosts, monitoring system logs and files for signs of compromise. Think of it as having a security guard inside your home, checking every room for intruders. Both types of IDS play a crucial role in identifying potential threats, but attackers have developed evasion techniques specific to each. Let's explore these evasion tactics and how to defend against them. One common evasion technique is fragmentation, where attackers split malicious payloads into smaller fragments to avoid detection by network-based IDS. It's like trying to sneak a large object past security by disassembling it into smaller, less conspicuous parts. To defend against fragmentation attacks, IDS should have robust reassembly mechanisms to piece together fragmented packets and analyze them as a whole. Another evasion method involves encoding or obfuscating malicious payloads to make them appear benign. Attackers use techniques like Base64 encoding or encryption to hide their intentions. It's like sending a message in a secret code that only the intended recipient can decipher. To detect such evasive payloads, IDS must be equipped with advanced decoding capabilities to uncover hidden threats. Polymorphic malware presents a unique challenge for IDS. Polymorphic code changes its appearance each time it's executed, making it challenging to identify based on signatures. It's like a chameleon that changes color to blend into its surroundings. To combat polymorphic malware, IDS should rely on behavior-based analysis rather than static signatures. Another evasion tactic involves evading host-based IDS by disabling or manipulating the logging mechanisms on compromised devices. Attackers can erase logs or inject fake entries to cover their tracks. It's like tampering with a security camera's recording to hide criminal activity. To defend against this evasion technique, it's crucial to implement proper log management and monitoring practices. Tunneling is a technique where attackers encapsulate malicious traffic within legitimate protocols, making it appear harmless to network-based IDS. It's like smuggling contraband inside a seemingly innocent package. To detect tunneling attacks, IDS should have the capability to inspect traffic within tunnels and identify anomalies. Evasion through encryption is a significant concern for IDS, as encrypted traffic conceals its content from analysis. Attackers can use secure protocols like HTTPS to encrypt malicious communication. It's like sealing a message in an impenetrable envelope. To combat this evasion tactic, IDS should employ decryption capabilities to inspect encrypted traffic for signs of malicious activity. Protocol evasion involves manipulating network protocols to bypass detection. Attackers can craft packets that exploit weaknesses in protocol implementations, making them difficult for IDS to interpret correctly. It's like using a secret handshake to gain entry to a private club. To defend against protocol evasion, IDS must have thorough protocol analysis capabilities and be able to identify anomalies. Attackers may also employ timing-based evasion techniques by adjusting the rate or timing of malicious activities to avoid triggering alarms. It's like sneaking through a laser security system by timing your movements precisely. To detect such subtle deviations,

IDS should incorporate sophisticated anomaly detection methods. Now, let's explore how to fortify your defenses against evasion techniques. Regularly updating IDS signatures and rules is crucial to ensure they can identify the latest threats. It's like giving your digital sentinels new instructions to recognize new forms of attack. Implementing a defense-in-depth strategy involves layering multiple security measures to catch malicious activities that might evade individual components. It's like having multiple layers of security guards at different points in a building. Utilizing threat intelligence feeds can provide real-time information about emerging threats and attack techniques. It's like receiving timely updates about criminal activities in your neighborhood. Behavior-based analysis is essential to identify deviations from normal network or host behavior. It's like having a keen observer who can spot unusual activities in a crowded area. Regularly auditing and monitoring IDS logs can help detect and investigate suspicious activities promptly. It's like reviewing security camera footage to identify potential intruders. Using anomaly detection methods can help identify subtle deviations that might evade signature-based detection. It's like noticing unusual behavior in a familiar environment. In summary, understanding evasion techniques is like being a vigilant security guard who knows how intruders might try to sneak past. While intrusion detection systems play a critical role in network security, attackers are constantly evolving their tactics. By staying informed about these evasion techniques and implementing robust defenses, you can enhance your network's resilience against threats. Just as a clever mouse evades the cat's grasp, a well-prepared defender can outsmart attackers and protect their digital domain. Stay vigilant, stay informed, and stay one step ahead in the ever-evolving landscape of cybersecurity.

Chapter 7: Post-Exploitation and Maintaining Access

Let's embark on a fascinating journey into the realm of covert communication channels in Wi-Fi attacks, where you'll uncover the clandestine methods used by attackers to exchange information under the radar, and how to defend against these covert channels. Imagine you're exploring the intricate world of espionage, where spies use covert codes and secret messages to communicate discreetly. In the realm of cybersecurity, understanding covert communication channels is like deciphering the hidden messages that attackers employ to operate in plain sight. Covert channels are communication pathways that evade detection by traditional security measures, allowing attackers to exchange information without raising suspicion. These channels are like underground tunnels for data, bypassing the regular traffic on the network. While Wi-Fi networks have become ubiquitous and essential for modern connectivity, they also offer opportunities for covert communication. To comprehend the significance of covert channels in Wi-Fi attacks, let's delve into how they work and the techniques attackers use to exploit them. Covert communication channels in Wi-Fi often exploit aspects of the network that are not typically monitored. One common method involves manipulating the service set identifier (SSID) of a Wi-Fi network. The SSID is like the name of a Wi-Fi network, and it's broadcasted so that devices can discover and connect to it. Attackers can alter the SSID to encode hidden information, such as commands or data. It's akin to writing a secret message in plain sight by rearranging the letters in a public sign. To detect and defend against this type of covert channel, Wi-Fi security tools should monitor SSID changes and anomalies. Another technique involves exploiting the timing and frequency of Wi-Fi packets to encode information. Attackers can subtly vary the timing between packets or the frequency of transmission to convey data. It's like sending Morse code through Wi-Fi signals, where the pauses and dots represent hidden messages. To counter this covert channel, monitoring tools should analyze packet timing and frequency patterns for anomalies. Covert channels can also operate in the frequency domain by modulating the amplitude or phase of Wi-Fi signals. Attackers can manipulate these aspects to encode information in a way that's imperceptible to ordinary users. It's similar to encoding a message in the variations of sound or light. To thwart this type of covert channel, Wi-Fi security solutions should inspect signal characteristics for irregularities. Steganography, the art of hiding data within other data, plays a significant role in covert communication channels. Attackers can embed data within seemingly innocent files or packets, making it difficult to detect. It's like concealing a message within a picture by subtly altering the colors of certain pixels. To detect steganographic covert channels, security tools should employ advanced pattern recognition and content analysis. Covert channels can also exploit unused or less-monitored aspects of Wi-Fi protocols. Attackers may manipulate reserved fields or control packets to convey hidden information. It's like using the white spaces in a book's margins to encode secret messages. To defend against this type of covert channel, security solutions should scrutinize Wi-Fi protocols thoroughly. The use of encrypted covert channels adds another layer of complexity to detection. Attackers can encrypt their hidden messages to evade standard inspection. It's like encoding a secret message in a language only known to the sender and receiver. To uncover encrypted covert channels, security tools must employ advanced decryption and analysis techniques. Now, let's explore strategies for defending against covert communication channels in Wi-Fi attacks. Implementing robust network monitoring and analysis tools is crucial to detect anomalies and deviations from normal Wi-Fi traffic. It's like having surveillance cameras that can spot unusual behavior in a crowded area. Regularly updating Wi-Fi security policies and configurations can help reduce vulnerabilities that attackers might exploit. It's like periodically reinforcing the locks on your doors to keep intruders out. Network segmentation and access controls can limit attackers' ability to move freely within a network, making it harder to establish covert channels. It's like dividing a large building into smaller compartments to prevent unauthorized access. Deep packet inspection and behavioral analysis can uncover hidden patterns and deviations associated with covert channels. It's like having an investigator who can detect subtle clues in a complex case. Employing intrusion detection and prevention systems (IDPS) can help identify and block covert communication channels as they emerge. It's like having a security guard who can intervene when suspicious activities are detected. Regular training and awareness programs for network administrators and users can help identify and report unusual network behavior. It's like educating a community to recognize and report suspicious activities in their neighborhood. In summary, understanding covert communication channels in Wi-Fi attacks is like deciphering a secret code that operates beneath the surface. While Wi-Fi networks are essential for modern connectivity, they can also be exploited by attackers seeking to exchange information covertly. By staying informed about these covert channel techniques and implementing robust defenses, you can enhance your network's resilience against threats. Just as a skilled detective uncovers hidden clues to solve a mystery, a vigilant defender can uncover and neutralize covert channels to protect their digital domain. Stay vigilant, stay informed, and stay one step ahead in the ever-evolving landscape of cybersecurity. Let's now delve into the intriguing topic of persistence mechanisms in wireless networks, where we'll explore how attackers maintain access to compromised networks over an extended period, and how defenders can thwart these persistent threats.

Think of persistence mechanisms as the ways in which attackers ensure their continued presence and control within a network, even after initial access has been achieved.

Imagine a persistent attacker as a crafty intruder who, once inside a building, finds secret hideaways to remain undetected while continuing their activities.

In the realm of cybersecurity, understanding these mechanisms is akin to identifying the hidden compartments and secret passages used by intruders to evade capture.

Persistence is a crucial element of cyberattacks, as attackers aim not only to breach a network but also to maintain their foothold for as long as possible.

Just as a skilled infiltrator might use hidden tunnels or secret doors to stay inside a building, cyber attackers employ various techniques to ensure they can return to compromised networks at will.

One common persistence mechanism is the use of backdoors, which are hidden entry points that allow attackers to access a system or network after their initial intrusion.

These backdoors can be like secret passages in a castle, known only to those with malicious intent.

To defend against backdoors, network administrators must conduct thorough security audits to identify and close any unauthorized access points.

Another technique attackers use for persistence is the installation of malicious software, often referred to as malware, that runs silently in the background.

This malware can be like a hidden spy within the network, allowing the attacker to maintain control and gather information without detection.

To combat this, robust antivirus and anti-malware solutions are essential, along with regular system scans.

Rootkits are another persistence mechanism that allows attackers to maintain control over a compromised system.

These are like invisible traps that can be challenging to detect and remove.

To counter rootkits, organizations should invest in rootkit detection tools and regularly update their systems.

Once attackers have established persistence, they often seek to maintain communication with compromised systems.

This communication is crucial for sending and receiving commands, exfiltrating data, or launching additional attacks.

Attackers may use covert channels within the network to maintain this communication, much like spies using secret codes.

To defend against these covert channels, network traffic must be closely monitored, and intrusion detection systems (IDS) should be configured to spot suspicious patterns.

Persistence mechanisms can also involve the use of scheduled tasks or cron jobs that execute malicious code at specific times or under certain conditions.

This scheduling can be like setting timers for actions that benefit the attacker.

To counter this, organizations should regularly review and manage scheduled tasks and cron jobs to identify any unauthorized or suspicious entries.

Registry modifications are another technique attackers employ to maintain persistence on Windows systems.

They may make changes to the Windows Registry, which is like the operating system's control center.

To protect against these modifications, organizations should implement robust system monitoring and auditing practices.

Attackers may also manipulate system services, altering their startup type to ensure they run automatically.

These services can be like the utilities in a building, and attackers may turn them into hidden tools for their purposes.

To defend against this, organizations should regularly review and audit system services.

Persistence can also be maintained through the use of hidden user accounts or privileges that grant attackers continued access.

These accounts and privileges can be like secret keys that open doors to unauthorized areas.

To counter this, organizations should regularly audit user accounts and privileges and implement the principle of least privilege.

Attackers often seek to blend in with legitimate network traffic to avoid detection while maintaining persistence.

This technique can be like an infiltrator wearing a disguise to move unnoticed within a crowd.

To detect and prevent this, network traffic should be monitored for anomalies and deviations from normal patterns.

Finally, attackers may use steganography to hide data within seemingly innocent files or communications.

This technique can be like encoding secret messages in plain sight.

To defend against steganography, organizations should employ advanced pattern recognition and content analysis.

In summary, understanding persistence mechanisms in wireless networks is like uncovering the hidden tricks employed by crafty intruders to maintain control over compromised systems.

While attackers aim to establish and maintain persistence for their malicious activities, defenders must remain vigilant and employ a combination of security measures.

By regularly auditing and monitoring systems, employing robust security tools, and staying informed about emerging threats, organizations can thwart persistent attackers and safeguard their digital domains.

Much like a diligent guardian, the key is to be proactive, adaptive, and always on the lookout for signs of persistent threats in the ever-evolving landscape of cybersecurity.

Chapter 8: Wireless Network Auditing Tools

Let's now explore the intriguing topic of covering tracks and forensic countermeasures in the world of cybersecurity, where we'll delve into the techniques used by attackers to hide their digital footprints and how defenders can uncover and analyze these hidden trails.

Imagine a digital detective scene, where an attacker attempts to erase all evidence of their presence, and cybersecurity professionals work tirelessly to piece together the clues left behind.

In the realm of cybersecurity, understanding covering tracks is like unraveling a mystery, and forensic countermeasures are the tools used to solve it.

Covering tracks, also known as anti-forensics, refers to the strategies and tactics employed by cyber attackers to conceal their activities and make it challenging for investigators to trace their steps.

It's akin to a master thief meticulously wiping away fingerprints and footprints at a crime scene.

These techniques can include erasing logs, altering timestamps, encrypting or obfuscating data, and even destroying or tampering with hardware.

The goal of covering tracks is to ensure that, even if an attacker's initial intrusion is detected, their identity and actions remain hidden.

Forensic countermeasures, on the other hand, are the methods and tools used by cybersecurity professionals to collect and analyze digital evidence, uncovering the truth behind cyberattacks.

Imagine forensic experts carefully collecting and preserving evidence at a crime scene to build a case.

In the world of cybersecurity, these experts use digital forensic techniques to reconstruct events, trace back to attackers, and gather evidence that can be used in legal proceedings.

Let's dive deeper into the world of covering tracks and the corresponding forensic countermeasures.

One common covering tracks technique is the manipulation or deletion of logs and records.

Attackers often attempt to erase their digital footprints by wiping out event logs, audit trails, and other records that might reveal their actions.

It's like a thief destroying security camera footage to avoid being identified.

To counter this, forensic experts use log analysis tools and backup systems to recover deleted or altered logs, uncovering the truth hidden within.

Another technique involves altering timestamps on files and logs to create false narratives about when certain actions occurred.

Attackers can make it appear as though their activities happened at different times or on different dates.

It's like an art forger altering the age of a painting to deceive art experts.

To combat this, digital forensic experts use timestamp analysis and synchronization to identify inconsistencies and determine the accurate timeline of events.

Encryption is another covering tracks method that attackers use to protect their data and communications from prying eyes.

By encrypting their files and communication, attackers aim to make it difficult for investigators to access and understand the information.

It's like locking a treasure chest with a complex puzzle, only solvable by those who possess the key.

To address this challenge, digital forensic specialists employ advanced decryption techniques and cryptographic analysis to uncover the encrypted content.

File obfuscation involves disguising files and data to make them appear benign or irrelevant.

Attackers may hide malicious code within seemingly harmless files, making it challenging for investigators to identify threats.

It's like hiding a valuable object within a collection of ordinary items.

Forensic experts counter this by using file analysis tools and signature-based detection to uncover hidden threats within obfuscated files.

Attackers may also employ rootkits and kernel-level techniques to maintain persistence and hide their presence.

Rootkits modify the core components of an operating system, making it difficult to detect their activities.

It's like a spy infiltrating the highest levels of an organization, operating in plain sight.

Forensic countermeasures involve rootkit detection tools and memory analysis to identify and remove these stealthy threats.

Memory analysis is a critical forensic technique used to examine the contents of a computer's memory (RAM) to identify running processes, open network connections, and artifacts left behind by attackers.

It's like searching for clues within the thoughts and actions of a suspect.

To combat this, forensic experts use memory forensics tools to reconstruct events and uncover hidden actions.

Network traffic analysis is another essential forensic countermeasure that involves monitoring and analyzing data packets on a network to identify anomalies and traces of malicious activity.

It's like studying the movements and interactions of individuals in a crowded marketplace.

Forensic analysts use packet capture and analysis tools to piece together the story of an attack and trace it back to its source.

Intrusion detection and prevention systems (IDPS) play a vital role in both covering tracks and forensic countermeasures.

Attackers may attempt to disable or evade IDPS to avoid detection, while defenders rely on these systems to identify and respond to threats.

It's like a game of cat and mouse between the attacker and the defender.

Forensic specialists use IDPS logs and alerts to reconstruct the timeline of an attack and understand how an attacker bypassed or disabled security measures.

In summary, the cat-and-mouse game of covering tracks and forensic countermeasures is like a digital detective story, where attackers aim to hide their actions, and cybersecurity professionals work diligently to uncover the truth.

Understanding the techniques used by attackers and the tools available to forensic experts is crucial in this ongoing battle.

By staying informed, employing advanced forensic techniques, and preserving evidence, defenders can unmask even the most elusive cybercriminals, ensuring that justice is served in the world of cybersecurity.

Let's delve into the exciting world of Wi-Fi penetration testing tools, where we'll explore the popular tools used by ethical hackers and security professionals to assess and strengthen the security of wireless networks.

Imagine you're equipped with a set of specialized tools, much like a locksmith with a collection of keys and picks, to assess the security of Wi-Fi networks.

In the realm of cybersecurity, these tools are the instruments that allow experts to uncover vulnerabilities and weaknesses in wireless networks.

Penetration testing, often referred to as ethical hacking, is a proactive approach to identifying and addressing security flaws before malicious actors can exploit them.

These Wi-Fi penetration testing tools are the virtual lockpicks and probes used by professionals to ensure the digital locks are secure.

One of the most popular Wi-Fi penetration testing tools is Aircrack-ng, a versatile and powerful suite of programs for assessing the security of Wi-Fi networks.

It's like having a Swiss Army knife for Wi-Fi security, with capabilities for capturing packets, cracking encryption keys, and conducting various attacks.

Wireshark is another essential tool for network analysis and packet sniffing, allowing security professionals to capture and examine network traffic.

Think of it as a magnifying glass for scrutinizing the data flowing through Wi-Fi networks, revealing any unusual or suspicious patterns.

Reaver is a specialized tool designed for testing the security of Wi-Fi Protected Setup (WPS) implementations.

WPS is like a shortcut for connecting devices to Wi-Fi networks, and Reaver is the tool that checks if it's secure or vulnerable to attacks.

Kismet is a powerful wireless network detector, sniffer, and intrusion detection system.

It's like a radar system that scans the airwaves for Wi-Fi signals and provides detailed information about nearby networks.

Hashcat is a robust password cracking tool that can be used for testing the strength of Wi-Fi passwords.

Imagine it as a digital locksmith's toolkit for testing how secure your Wi-Fi network's keys are.

Fern Wi-Fi Cracker is a user-friendly, GUI-based tool that simplifies Wi-Fi penetration testing.

It's like having a user-friendly interface to access all the lockpicking tools in your cybersecurity toolbox.

In addition to these tools, there are many others available, each with its specific purpose and capabilities.

For instance, Wifite is a Python script that automates Wi-Fi penetration testing, making it easier and more efficient for security professionals.

Think of it as a robotic assistant that takes care of repetitive tasks in the testing process.

Pyrit is a GPU-accelerated Wi-Fi cracking tool, harnessing the power of graphics cards to accelerate password cracking.

It's like having a high-speed sports car for Wi-Fi password recovery.

WifiPhisher is a social engineering tool that tricks users into connecting to malicious Wi-Fi networks.

It's like a digital illusionist that lures unsuspecting users into revealing their secrets.

Eaphammer is a tool for performing targeted evil twin attacks against WPA2-Enterprise networks.

Think of it as a digital chameleon that mimics legitimate networks to deceive and infiltrate.

These Wi-Fi penetration testing tools serve different purposes and cater to various skill levels, from beginners to seasoned professionals.

Just as a locksmith has a range of tools for different locks and scenarios, cybersecurity experts choose the right tool for the job at hand.

When conducting a Wi-Fi penetration test, it's crucial to have a well-defined scope and permission to test the network.

Imagine it as a locksmith being hired to assess the security of a specific building with the owner's consent.

Once the scope is established, security professionals use these tools to simulate attacks and identify vulnerabilities.

They might attempt to crack Wi-Fi passwords, launch deauthentication attacks, or test for WPS vulnerabilities.

It's like a locksmith trying different techniques to see if a lock can be picked or bypassed.

The goal is to uncover weaknesses in the network's defenses and provide recommendations for improvement.

Much like a locksmith recommending stronger locks or security measures for a building.

Penetration testers also assess the network's configuration, checking for misconfigurations that could lead to security breaches.

They might examine firewall rules, access control lists, and encryption settings to ensure they meet best practices.

It's like a locksmith inspecting the doorframe, hinges, and security system to ensure everything is in order. Once the assessment is complete, security professionals compile their findings and provide a detailed report to the network owner.

This report includes vulnerabilities discovered, potential risks, and recommendations for mitigating the identified issues. It's like a locksmith delivering a report outlining the weaknesses in a building's security and suggesting improvements.

In summary, Wi-Fi penetration testing tools are the essential instruments that cybersecurity professionals use to assess and enhance the security of wireless networks.

These tools are like the lockpicks, probes, and keys in a locksmith's toolkit, allowing experts to uncover vulnerabilities and strengthen digital locks.

Penetration testing is a proactive approach to identifying and addressing security flaws, much like a locksmith ensuring that a building's locks are secure.

By using these tools, professionals can simulate attacks, identify weaknesses, and provide recommendations for improving Wi-Fi network security.

Much like a locksmith recommending stronger locks and security measures, their goal is to safeguard the digital domains we rely on in our increasingly connected world.

Chapter 9: Social Engineering in Wi-Fi Hacking

Let's explore the fascinating and often unsettling world of psychological manipulation in the context of social engineering, where individuals with malicious intent use psychological tactics to manipulate and deceive others for personal gain.

Imagine a skilled illusionist, not performing magic tricks on a stage, but rather weaving intricate webs of deception in the digital realm.

In the realm of cybersecurity, social engineering is the art of manipulating human psychology to exploit vulnerabilities in an individual's or organization's security defenses.

It's akin to a digital con artist using charm and persuasion to trick people into revealing sensitive information or performing actions they wouldn't typically do.

Psychological manipulation is a key component of social engineering, as it involves understanding how people think, feel, and react to certain stimuli.

These manipulative techniques are the tools that social engineers use to influence their targets.

One of the fundamental principles of psychological manipulation is the concept of trust.

Social engineers often work to establish trust with their targets, creating a sense of rapport and credibility.

This trust-building phase can involve mirroring the target's behavior, interests, and values, making the target feel more comfortable and less suspicious.

It's like a skilled actor taking on a role that aligns perfectly with the expectations of the audience.

Another powerful technique in the arsenal of social engineers is the exploitation of cognitive biases.

Cognitive biases are inherent shortcuts in human thinking that can lead to irrational decisions and actions.

Social engineers leverage these biases to manipulate their targets.

For example, the scarcity bias can be exploited by creating a sense of urgency or limited availability to encourage immediate action.

It's like a salesperson saying, "This offer is only available today," to prompt a quick purchase decision.

Reciprocity is another cognitive bias that social engineers tap into. People tend to feel obliged to return a favor when someone has done something nice for them.

Social engineers may offer assistance or information as a way to create a sense of indebtedness.

It's like a neighbor who lends you a hand with a task, expecting you'll return the favor in the future.

Authority is a psychological principle that social engineers often utilize. People tend to follow the lead of experts or authoritative figures.

By posing as an authority figure or someone with expertise, social engineers can manipulate their targets into compliance.

It's like a person impersonating a police officer, making others more likely to follow their instructions.

The concept of social proof is another potent psychological tool in the social engineer's kit. People tend to follow the crowd and do what others are doing.

Social engineers may create fake testimonials, reviews, or endorsements to give the illusion of popular support for their actions.

It's like a restaurant with an empty dining room that places a few actors at tables to make it look busy.

Fear and intimidation are tactics that some social engineers employ to manipulate their targets.

By instilling fear of negative consequences or harm, they can pressure individuals into taking actions they wouldn't otherwise.

It's like a scammer threatening to expose embarrassing information unless a victim complies.

Another psychological manipulation technique is the use of baiting, where the social engineer dangles a tempting offer or opportunity to lure the target into a trap.

This can involve offering free software downloads, enticing email attachments, or fake job opportunities.

It's like a fisherman using a shiny lure to attract unsuspecting fish.

Pretexting is a form of social engineering that involves creating a fabricated scenario or pretext to gain the trust and cooperation of the target.

Social engineers may pose as coworkers, service personnel, or authorities to extract information or access.

It's like an actor playing a role in a play, convincing the audience with a convincing performance.

Phishing, one of the most prevalent forms of social engineering, relies on deception and psychological manipulation.

Phishers use fake emails, websites, or messages to trick recipients into revealing sensitive information, such as login credentials or financial data.

It's like a magician distracting the audience's attention while performing a sleight of hand trick.

Vishing, or voice phishing, is another variant of social engineering that uses phone calls to manipulate targets.

Social engineers may impersonate legitimate organizations or individuals to extract information or funds over the phone.

It's like a ventriloquist using their voice to make it seem like an inanimate object is speaking.

In summary, psychological manipulation is the dark art of social engineering, where individuals use cunning tactics to exploit the vulnerabilities of human psychology.

Understanding these techniques is crucial for individuals and organizations to protect themselves against manipulation and deception.

Just as a magician reveals the secrets behind their tricks to educate the audience, demystifying psychological manipulation empowers us to recognize and resist the tactics employed by social engineers.

By becoming aware of these psychological ploys and remaining vigilant, we can better safeguard our digital lives and personal information in an increasingly interconnected world.

Let's delve into the world of phishing and impersonation attacks in the context of Wi-Fi networks, where cybercriminals employ deceptive tactics to trick users into revealing sensitive information or gaining unauthorized access.

Imagine you're walking through a crowded marketplace, and a charming vendor offers you what appears to be a valuable item at an unbelievably low price.

In the realm of cybersecurity, phishing and impersonation attacks are like those deceptive vendors, attempting to lure unsuspecting users with enticing offers and promises.

Phishing is a form of cyberattack where malicious actors impersonate trustworthy entities, such as banks, social media platforms, or government agencies, to deceive users into revealing sensitive information like login credentials, credit card numbers, or personal data.

It's akin to an online con artist disguising themselves as a legitimate entity to gain your trust.

In Wi-Fi networks, phishing attacks can take on various forms. One common method is email phishing, where users receive fraudulent emails that appear to come from a reputable source.

These emails often contain links to fake websites that closely mimic the appearance of legitimate ones, aiming to capture login information.

Imagine receiving an email that appears to be from your bank, asking you to verify your account by clicking on a link. This is a classic phishing attempt.

Spear phishing is a more targeted variant of phishing, where cybercriminals tailor their attacks to specific individuals or organizations.

They gather information about their targets, such as their interests, job titles, or connections, to craft highly convincing and personalized phishing messages.

It's like a skilled actor studying their role in great detail to deliver a convincing performance.

In Wi-Fi networks, spear phishing attacks may involve creating rogue Wi-Fi hotspots with names that appear to be associated with a trusted organization, enticing victims to connect.

Vishing, or voice phishing, is another phishing technique that uses phone calls to deceive targets. Cybercriminals impersonate legitimate organizations or authorities over the phone to extract sensitive information.

Imagine receiving a call from someone claiming to be a tech support agent, urgently requesting access to your computer to resolve a supposed issue. This is an example of vishing.

Impersonation attacks in Wi-Fi networks involve malicious actors posing as legitimate access points or devices to intercept network traffic or deceive users.

One common impersonation attack is the evil twin attack, where cybercriminals set up a rogue access point with a name similar to a legitimate one, tricking users into connecting.

Imagine you're at a coffee shop, and you see two available Wi-Fi networks: "CoffeeShopGuest" and "CoffeeShopGuest_2." You may unwittingly connect to the rogue access point, giving cybercriminals access to your data.

Another impersonation attack is the man-in-the-middle (MitM) attack, where an attacker intercepts and possibly alters communication between two parties without their knowledge.

In Wi-Fi networks, this could involve an attacker positioning themselves between a user's device and a legitimate access point, allowing them to eavesdrop on or manipulate the data being exchanged.

It's like a clever spy intercepting secret messages between two agents and altering the content.

To protect against phishing and impersonation attacks in Wi-Fi networks, users should exercise caution and follow best practices.

Always verify the legitimacy of emails and messages, especially if they request sensitive information or contain suspicious links.

Check for signs of phishing, such as misspelled URLs or email addresses, and use two-factor authentication whenever possible.

When connecting to Wi-Fi networks, be cautious of open or unsecured networks and avoid connecting to access points with names that seem suspicious or similar to known networks.

Consider using a virtual private network (VPN) to encrypt your internet traffic, adding an extra layer of security when using public Wi-Fi.

Educate yourself and your employees about phishing and impersonation tactics, emphasizing the importance of skepticism and vigilance.

In the ever-evolving landscape of cyber threats, staying informed and proactive is key to protecting yourself and your organization from phishing and impersonation attacks.

Just as you'd be cautious when encountering a charming vendor in a bustling marketplace, exercising caution and awareness in the digital world will help safeguard your personal information and privacy from cybercriminals who seek to deceive and exploit.

Chapter 10: Legal and Ethical Considerations in Penetration Testing

Navigating the complex landscape of compliance and regulatory requirements is essential in today's interconnected world.

Imagine you're embarking on a journey, and each regulatory requirement is like a signpost on the path, guiding you toward responsible and secure practices.

Compliance refers to adhering to specific rules, standards, and guidelines established by governments, industries, or organizations to ensure that certain criteria are met.

These criteria often relate to security, privacy, data protection, and ethical conduct.

One of the most well-known regulatory frameworks is the General Data Protection Regulation (GDPR), which governs the protection of personal data for individuals within the European Union.

GDPR sets stringent rules for how organizations collect, store, and process personal data, and it imposes hefty fines for non-compliance.

Imagine you're the guardian of sensitive information, and GDPR is your trusty shield, ensuring that data is handled with care.

The Health Insurance Portability and Accountability Act (HIPAA) is another significant regulatory framework, specifically targeting the healthcare industry in the United States.

HIPAA mandates strict rules for safeguarding patients' medical records and information, aiming to protect their privacy and ensure the security of healthcare data.

Think of HIPAA as a guardian angel watching over your medical history, keeping it safe and confidential.

Payment Card Industry Data Security Standard (PCI DSS) is crucial for organizations that handle credit card information.

PCI DSS establishes security requirements to protect cardholder data and prevent data breaches, safeguarding sensitive financial information.

Imagine PCI DSS as a vigilant sentinel ensuring the security of your credit card transactions.

Regulatory requirements vary across industries and regions, and they often evolve to address emerging threats and technologies.

For example, in the financial sector, the Basel III framework sets capital requirements for banks to ensure stability in the banking system.

Think of Basel III as a safety net, preventing financial institutions from toppling over in times of economic turbulence.

In the realm of cybersecurity, compliance with regulatory standards is vital to protect sensitive data and maintain the trust of customers and partners.

Compliance is not just about avoiding penalties; it's also about demonstrating a commitment to security and ethical conduct.

Picture it as a badge of honor, showcasing your dedication to safeguarding information.

Regulatory requirements can be a complex web of rules and obligations, but they serve a crucial purpose in our digital age.

They help build trust, protect individuals' rights, and create a level playing field for businesses and organizations.

Now, let's explore the process of achieving and maintaining compliance.

The first step is to identify the relevant regulations and standards that apply to your organization based on its industry, location, and the type of data it handles.

Imagine this step as mapping out the terrain before embarking on a journey to ensure you're on the right path.

Once you've identified the applicable regulations, the next step is to assess your organization's current practices and systems to determine compliance gaps.

Think of this as a self-audit, where you examine your processes to see if they align with the regulatory requirements.

Now, you'll need to create a compliance roadmap, outlining the steps and actions required to bridge those gaps.

This roadmap is your guide, showing you the way forward and helping you set priorities.

Implementing the necessary changes and controls is the heart of the compliance journey.

It's like building a sturdy bridge to cross a challenging river, ensuring that your organization can safely navigate the regulatory landscape.

Training and awareness programs are essential to ensure that your employees understand their roles and responsibilities in maintaining compliance.

Think of it as equipping your team with the knowledge and tools they need for a successful expedition.

Regular monitoring and auditing of your compliance efforts are crucial to identify any issues or deviations from the regulatory requirements.

Imagine this as regularly checking your compass to ensure you're still on the right path.

In the event of non-compliance or security incidents, having a response and remediation plan in place is vital to address the situation swiftly and effectively.

Think of it as an emergency kit that helps you navigate unexpected challenges along the way.

Compliance is an ongoing journey, not a one-time destination.

Regulatory requirements evolve, and your organization must adapt to stay in compliance.

Think of it as a perpetual expedition where you continue to navigate the changing landscape.

Maintaining compliance requires dedication, resources, and a commitment to upholding the values and principles that underpin regulatory frameworks.

It's like tending to a garden, where regular care and attention yield a bountiful harvest of security and trust.

In summary, compliance and regulatory requirements are integral to our modern digital world.

They provide a framework for safeguarding data, protecting privacy, and ensuring ethical conduct.

Navigating this landscape is like embarking on an expedition, where each regulation is a signpost guiding us toward responsible and secure practices.

Achieving and maintaining compliance is a journey that requires diligence, adaptability, and a commitment to upholding the principles of security and trust.

Just as explorers of old relied on maps and compasses to navigate uncharted territories, organizations rely on compliance frameworks to navigate the complex landscape of cybersecurity and data protection.

Reporting and disclosure guidelines play a crucial role in the realm of ethical hacking, ensuring that security vulnerabilities are addressed responsibly and transparently.

Imagine you're a vigilant watchdog, keenly observing potential weaknesses in a system, ready to bark if you sense danger.

Ethical hackers, often referred to as white-hat hackers, are individuals or cybersecurity professionals who engage in authorized hacking activities to identify and address vulnerabilities in computer systems, networks, or applications.

They are the digital protectors of the cyber realm, safeguarding it from malicious actors.

When an ethical hacker discovers a security vulnerability during their testing or assessment, the first step is to accurately document their findings.

Imagine this as taking detailed notes, recording every aspect of the vulnerability, including its nature, location, and potential impact.

Effective documentation is like building a case file, providing a comprehensive view of the vulnerability for later analysis and action.

Once the vulnerability is documented, the ethical hacker must assess its severity and potential impact.

This evaluation involves considering how an attacker could exploit the vulnerability and what consequences it could have for the organization.

Think of it as assessing the potential damage that a security breach could cause.

Ethical hackers often use standardized scoring systems, such as the Common Vulnerability Scoring System (CVSS), to assign a severity score to the vulnerability.

These scores help organizations prioritize and address vulnerabilities based on their criticality.

Imagine it as giving a threat level to a potential danger, so everyone knows how serious it is.

Now comes the crucial part: reporting the vulnerability to the organization or entity that owns or operates the system.

Ethical hackers must follow a responsible disclosure process, which involves notifying the organization about the vulnerability without revealing sensitive details publicly.

Think of it as alerting the building owner about a weak lock on their door without broadcasting it to potential burglars.

Responsible disclosure allows organizations to take prompt action to fix the vulnerability and protect their systems and data.

Ethical hackers often provide a detailed report to the organization, including technical information about the vulnerability, its potential impact, and steps to reproduce it.

Imagine this report as a roadmap that guides the organization toward resolving the issue.

Upon receiving the report, the organization's security team or IT department takes action to validate the vulnerability and assess its accuracy.

They may conduct their own testing to confirm the findings of the ethical hacker.

This step is like a second opinion from a medical specialist to ensure the diagnosis is correct.

Once the organization has verified the vulnerability, they work on developing a patch or solution to address it.

Imagine this as a team of builders fixing a structural issue in a building to make it safe and secure.

During this process, communication between the ethical hacker and the organization is essential.

The hacker may provide guidance and clarifications to help the organization understand the vulnerability better and develop an effective solution.

This collaboration is like a detective working alongside the building owner to strengthen security.

Once a solution or patch is developed, the organization deploys it to mitigate the vulnerability.

Imagine it as reinforcing the building's security by adding better locks and alarms.

After implementing the solution, the organization conducts thorough testing to ensure that the vulnerability is effectively addressed and that no new issues are introduced.

This step is like stress-testing the building's security measures to ensure they work flawlessly.

Finally, the organization notifies the ethical hacker of the resolution and may express their gratitude for helping improve their security.

This cooperative relationship between the hacker and the organization is akin to teamwork in ensuring the safety of a community.

The entire process, from discovery to resolution, follows ethical principles and guidelines to protect both the organization and the ethical hacker.

It's like a code of conduct that ensures responsible and transparent practices.

One key aspect of responsible disclosure is setting a reasonable timeframe for the organization to address the vulnerability.

This timeframe allows the organization to prioritize and allocate resources effectively.

Imagine it as giving the building owner a reasonable deadline to fix the weak lock on their door.

If the organization fails to address the vulnerability within a reasonable timeframe or does not respond to the disclosure, the ethical hacker may consider responsible disclosure to be unsuccessful.

In such cases, the hacker may choose to publicly disclose the vulnerability to raise awareness and put pressure on the organization to take action.

Think of it as alerting the neighborhood about the security risk posed by a building with a weak lock.

However, public disclosure is often considered a last resort, as it can potentially expose users to risks before a solution is in place.

In the world of ethical hacking, reporting and disclosure guidelines ensure that security vulnerabilities are addressed in a responsible and transparent manner.

Ethical hackers act as digital protectors, alerting organizations to potential risks and helping them strengthen their security measures.

Their cooperative efforts with organizations result in safer digital environments for everyone.

Just as a vigilant watchdog alerts its owner to potential dangers, ethical hackers play a vital role in safeguarding the digital world from cyber threats.

BOOK 3
ADVANCED WIRELESS EXPLOITATION
A COMPREHENSIVE GUIDE TO PENETRATION TESTING

ROB BOTWRIGHT

Chapter 1: Advanced Wireless Network Security Overview

Navigating the ever-evolving threat landscape in wireless security is akin to exploring a dynamic and sometimes treacherous terrain.

Imagine it as setting sail on a ship, constantly scanning the horizon for potential storms and dangers.

In recent years, wireless technology has become an integral part of our daily lives, enabling seamless connectivity and convenience.

Wireless networks have expanded rapidly, from home Wi-Fi to large-scale corporate deployments and public hotspots.

Think of it as weaving a vast web of interconnected devices, allowing data to flow effortlessly.

However, with this convenience comes a heightened risk, as cybercriminals are constantly seeking vulnerabilities to exploit.

Picture them as opportunistic pirates, ready to board any vulnerable ship.

One of the prominent threats in wireless security is the proliferation of unsecured or poorly secured Wi-Fi networks.

Imagine leaving the door to your house wide open, inviting anyone to enter and access your personal space.

Similarly, open and unsecured Wi-Fi networks invite unauthorized users to intercept data, engage in malicious activities, and compromise network security.

Another growing concern is the rise of man-in-the-middle (MITM) attacks on wireless networks.

Think of these attacks as eavesdroppers intercepting your conversations, but in the digital realm.

MITM attackers position themselves between the user and the target, intercepting and possibly altering the communication.

These attacks can occur in various forms, from intercepting sensitive data to injecting malicious code into legitimate traffic.

Moreover, rogue access points pose a significant threat in wireless security.

Imagine someone setting up a fake checkpoint on the road, diverting unsuspecting travelers from their intended path.

Rogue access points impersonate legitimate Wi-Fi networks, tricking users into connecting to them.

Once connected, cybercriminals can intercept data, launch attacks, and compromise user devices.

Password-related vulnerabilities remain a persistent concern in wireless security.

Weak and easily guessable passwords are like leaving the keys to your house under the doormat.

Cybercriminals can use brute-force attacks or exploit default credentials to gain unauthorized access to Wi-Fi networks and connected devices.

Additionally, the advent of the Internet of Things (IoT) has introduced new security challenges.

Imagine a bustling city with various types of vehicles, each requiring different traffic rules and safety measures.

IoT devices come in various shapes and sizes, often lacking robust security features.

These devices can be compromised and used as entry points to infiltrate the broader network.

Cybercriminals can exploit vulnerabilities in IoT devices to gain access to sensitive data and control critical systems.

Wireless security also faces threats from the growing sophistication of attacks.

Imagine a group of thieves upgrading from simple lock-picking tools to high-tech electronic devices.

Cybercriminals are using advanced techniques such as zero-day exploits, polymorphic malware, and evasion tactics to bypass security measures.

These techniques make it challenging to detect and defend against attacks.

Furthermore, insider threats pose a significant risk in wireless security.

Imagine a trusted colleague turning out to be a spy for the enemy.

Insiders with access to the network can intentionally or unintentionally compromise security by sharing sensitive information or falling victim to social engineering attacks.

The threat landscape is not limited to Wi-Fi networks alone; cellular networks are also vulnerable.

Think of them as interconnected highways, with different carriers and technologies running alongside each other.

Mobile devices can be targeted with malware, phishing attacks, and SIM swapping schemes, putting users at risk.

With the advent of 5G technology, the attack surface is expected to expand, creating new security challenges.

As the threat landscape continues to evolve, organizations and individuals must adopt proactive security measures to protect their wireless networks and devices.

Imagine these measures as fortifications and watchtowers, ensuring that your digital castle remains secure.

Implementing strong encryption protocols, regularly updating software and firmware, and conducting security assessments are essential steps in mitigating risks.

Additionally, user education and awareness play a crucial role in wireless security.

Think of it as equipping travelers with knowledge of potential dangers and safe practices on their journey.

Users should be trained to recognize phishing attempts, avoid connecting to unsecured networks, and practice good password hygiene.

Collaboration among security professionals, researchers, and organizations is vital in staying ahead of emerging threats.

Imagine it as a network of allies, sharing intelligence and strategies to defend against common adversaries.

The current threat landscape in wireless security is ever-changing, but with vigilance, education, and collaboration, individuals and organizations can navigate this terrain and safeguard their digital assets.

Just as explorers of old relied on maps and knowledge of the terrain to navigate uncharted territories, modern-day users and organizations rely on cybersecurity practices to navigate the evolving landscape of wireless security.

As we delve into the realm of Wi-Fi security, it's essential to understand that the landscape is not static; it's a dynamic and ever-evolving domain.

Think of it as a constantly changing puzzle, where new pieces are added, and the picture keeps shifting.

One of the emerging challenges in Wi-Fi security is the increasing complexity of network environments.

Imagine your Wi-Fi network as a jigsaw puzzle with numerous pieces, each representing a different device or technology.

With the proliferation of IoT devices, BYOD (Bring Your Own Device) policies, and hybrid work models, managing and securing this puzzle becomes more intricate.

Another trend is the growing reliance on cloud-based services and remote work.

Picture your Wi-Fi network as a bridge connecting you to the cloud, where your data and applications reside.

This trend has introduced new attack vectors, as cybercriminals seek to exploit vulnerabilities in cloud services and remote access points.

The adoption of Wi-Fi 6, the latest generation of Wi-Fi technology, is another noteworthy development.

Think of it as upgrading from a bicycle to a high-speed sports car in terms of network performance.

While Wi-Fi 6 brings improved speed and efficiency, it also presents new security considerations, such as potential vulnerabilities in the protocol.

Additionally, the widespread use of public Wi-Fi hotspots continues to be a challenge.

Imagine these hotspots as bustling public squares, where many individuals gather to connect to the internet.

These networks are often unsecured, making users vulnerable to eavesdropping and other cyber threats.

Cybercriminals can set up rogue hotspots to lure unsuspecting users into connecting, leading to potential security breaches.

Moreover, the rise of advanced and persistent threats poses a significant challenge.

Think of these threats as elusive and persistent adversaries, constantly probing for weaknesses in your defenses.

These attackers use sophisticated techniques to bypass security measures and gain unauthorized access to networks.

Phishing attacks have also evolved, becoming more targeted and convincing.

Picture phishing emails as baited traps, designed to look like genuine communications from trusted sources.

These attacks aim to deceive users into revealing sensitive information or clicking on malicious links.

The use of artificial intelligence and machine learning in cyberattacks is a growing trend.

Imagine cybercriminals as using advanced tools that learn and adapt, making them more effective at evading detection.

These technologies can automate tasks like reconnaissance, making attacks faster and more efficient.

The shift to a Zero Trust security model is gaining traction in response to these evolving challenges.

Think of Zero Trust as a "trust no one" approach, where every user and device must be verified and authenticated, even if they are within the network perimeter.

This model aims to minimize the attack surface and enhance security.

The concept of secure access service edge (SASE) is also becoming prominent.

Picture SASE as a security umbrella that extends over your network and cloud resources.

It integrates network and security functions, providing a unified and streamlined approach to protection.

Furthermore, privacy concerns and data protection regulations are influencing Wi-Fi security practices.

Imagine these regulations as guardrails, ensuring that data is handled responsibly and ethically.

Organizations must comply with laws like GDPR and CCPA, which require robust security measures and data breach reporting.

In response to these challenges and trends, the role of security professionals is evolving.

Think of them as the guardians of your digital realm, adapting their skills and strategies to address new threats.

They must stay informed about emerging threats, continuously update security measures, and educate users about safe practices.

Collaboration and information sharing among security professionals and organizations are essential.

Picture it as a network of guardians working together to strengthen the collective defense against cyber threats.

In summary, navigating the ever-changing landscape of Wi-Fi security requires adaptability and vigilance.

Think of it as a journey through uncharted territory, where each challenge and trend shapes the path ahead.

By staying informed, adopting new security models, and fostering collaboration, individuals and organizations can effectively address emerging challenges and trends in Wi-Fi security.

Just as explorers adapt to changing landscapes and climates, security professionals and users must adapt to the evolving terrain of Wi-Fi security to protect their digital assets and data.

Chapter 2: Deep Dive into Wi-Fi Protocols and Standards

Understanding the various Wi-Fi protocols is like unraveling the layers of a technological onion.

Imagine each layer as a distinct chapter in a fascinating story of wireless communication.

Wi-Fi protocols are the rules and standards that govern how wireless devices communicate over radio waves.

Picture them as the grammar and vocabulary of a language spoken by your devices.

The earliest Wi-Fi protocol, known as 802.11, emerged in the late 1990s.

Think of it as the foundation upon which modern Wi-Fi technology was built.

It provided a modest data rate of 2 Mbps and operated in the 2.4 GHz frequency band.

This protocol enabled basic wireless connectivity but lacked the speed and robustness needed for today's demands.

As technology advanced, so did Wi-Fi protocols, giving birth to 802.11b, the first widely adopted high-speed protocol.

Imagine it as a turbocharged engine that propelled wireless networks forward.

802.11b offered a data rate of up to 11 Mbps, making it a significant improvement over its predecessor.

However, it still operated in the crowded 2.4 GHz band, leading to potential interference issues.

802.11g came next, building upon the foundation of 802.11b.

Think of it as adding more lanes to a highway to accommodate faster traffic.

This protocol increased the data rate to 54 Mbps while maintaining compatibility with 802.11b devices.

It also operated in the 2.4 GHz band, which was becoming increasingly congested.

The 802.11a protocol took a different approach, envisioning a new express lane on a parallel road.

Imagine it as a separate highway operating in the less crowded 5 GHz band.

802.11a offered a data rate of up to 54 Mbps, making it suitable for high-bandwidth applications.

However, it was not backward compatible with 802.11b, leading to compatibility challenges.

802.11n arrived as a game-changer, combining the best of both worlds.

Picture it as a multi-lane highway that accommodates various types of traffic.

This protocol supported both 2.4 GHz and 5 GHz bands and introduced MIMO (Multiple Input, Multiple Output) technology.

802.11n offered data rates up to 600 Mbps, significantly improving wireless performance.

The 802.11ac protocol marked another leap in Wi-Fi evolution.

Think of it as the introduction of fiber-optic lines on the information highway.

802.11ac operated exclusively in the 5 GHz band, providing data rates exceeding 1 Gbps.

It introduced features like beamforming and wider channel widths for improved performance.

802.11ax, also known as Wi-Fi 6, emerged as the latest and most advanced protocol.

Imagine it as a futuristic highway with intelligent traffic management.

Wi-Fi 6 operates in both 2.4 GHz and 5 GHz bands and offers data rates surpassing 10 Gbps.

It incorporates technologies like OFDMA (Orthogonal Frequency Division Multiple Access) and MU-MIMO (Multi-User, Multiple Input, Multiple Output) for increased efficiency in crowded environments.

Now, consider the security aspect of Wi-Fi protocols.

Think of it as building strong locks and gates to protect your data.

WEP (Wired Equivalent Privacy) was the first security protocol for Wi-Fi, but it had significant vulnerabilities.

Imagine it as a lock that could be easily picked.

WPA (Wi-Fi Protected Access) replaced WEP with a more robust security mechanism.

Picture it as a sturdier lock that required more effort to break.

WPA2 further enhanced security, making it the standard for many years.

Think of it as a high-security vault protecting your valuable data.

However, vulnerabilities like KRACK (Key Reinstallation Attack) exposed weaknesses in WPA2.

WPA3, the latest security protocol, aims to strengthen Wi-Fi security.

Imagine it as a state-of-the-art security system with advanced encryption and protection against brute-force attacks.

WPA3 introduces features like individualized data encryption and protection against offline dictionary attacks.

Understanding these protocols is crucial for optimizing Wi-Fi performance and ensuring data security.

Think of it as having the right tools to navigate the wireless landscape effectively.

Choosing the appropriate Wi-Fi protocol depends on factors like device compatibility, network requirements, and security considerations.

Picture it as selecting the right vehicle for a specific journey.

Each protocol has its strengths and weaknesses, and the choice should align with your specific needs.

Considerations like the number of devices, network congestion, and desired data rates play a significant role.

Imagine it as customizing your vehicle for a particular road trip.

For example, Wi-Fi 6 is ideal for environments with numerous devices and high data demands.

On the other hand, older protocols like 802.11n may suffice for less demanding scenarios.

Think of it as selecting the right tool for the job, whether it's a sports car for speed or a utility vehicle for versatility.

In summary, Wi-Fi protocols are the building blocks of wireless communication, defining how devices communicate and secure data.

Picture them as the language of wireless technology, enabling seamless connectivity and protecting your digital world.

Understanding the evolution of these protocols and their unique features empowers you to make informed choices for your wireless network.

Think of it as having a comprehensive map to navigate the ever-expanding landscape of Wi-Fi technology, ensuring a smooth and secure journey for your devices and data.

Embarking on a journey through the evolution of Wi-Fi standards is like tracing the footsteps of technological progress.

Imagine it as a captivating narrative that unfolds chapter by chapter, revealing how wireless communication has transformed over the years.

Our story begins in the early 1990s, a time when the idea of wireless connectivity was still in its infancy.

Picture a world where wired connections dominated, and the concept of a wireless local area network (WLAN) was just beginning to take shape.

In this era, the first chapter introduces us to IEEE 802.11, the foundation upon which all Wi-Fi standards are built.

Think of it as the blueprint for wireless communication, outlining the basic rules and protocols.

802.11's initial incarnation offered a mere 2 Mbps data rate and operated in the 2.4 GHz frequency band.

Imagine it as a tentative first step into the world of wireless, with limited capabilities and a narrow bandwidth.

As technology advanced, our story moves to the second chapter, where we encounter 802.11b.

Consider this as the moment when Wi-Fi gained its first taste of speed.

802.11b increased the data rate to 11 Mbps, making it a significant improvement over its predecessor.

Think of it as the transition from a leisurely stroll to a brisk walk in the world of wireless connectivity.

However, 802.11b still operated within the crowded 2.4 GHz band, leading to potential interference issues.

Chapter three introduces us to 802.11a, a protocol that ventured into a new territory—the 5 GHz frequency band.

Imagine it as opening a new avenue of possibilities, free from the congestion of 2.4 GHz.

802.11a offered a data rate of up to 54 Mbps, making it suitable for high-bandwidth applications.

Yet, it wasn't backward compatible with 802.11b, posing challenges in terms of interoperability.

Chapter four brings us to 802.11g, a protocol that aimed to bridge the gap between 802.11b and 802.11a.

Think of it as a harmonious blend of the best features from its predecessors.

802.11g maintained compatibility with 802.11b devices while offering a data rate of 54 Mbps.

However, it still operated primarily within the crowded 2.4 GHz band, facing potential interference.

As our story progresses, we arrive at the fifth chapter, where we encounter 802.11n—a true game-changer.

Imagine it as the moment when Wi-Fi transformed from a leisurely walk to a brisk run.

802.11n supported both 2.4 GHz and 5 GHz bands and introduced MIMO (Multiple Input, Multiple Output) technology.

This protocol provided data rates of up to 600 Mbps, significantly improving wireless performance.

Chapter six introduces us to 802.11ac, a protocol that embraced the 5 GHz band exclusively.

Think of it as the leap into the express lane of the wireless highway.

802.11ac shattered previous speed records, offering data rates exceeding 1 Gbps.

It also introduced features like beamforming and wider channel widths for improved performance.

As we move forward, we arrive at the seventh chapter, where Wi-Fi 6 takes center stage as 802.11ax.

Imagine it as the dawn of a new era, marked by unprecedented speed and efficiency.

Wi-Fi 6 operates in both 2.4 GHz and 5 GHz bands and offers data rates surpassing 10 Gbps.

This protocol incorporates technologies like OFDMA (Orthogonal Frequency Division Multiple Access) and MU-MIMO (Multi-User, Multiple Input, Multiple Output) for increased efficiency in crowded environments.

Throughout this journey, it's essential to grasp the significance of backward compatibility.

Consider it as the ability of new Wi-Fi standards to communicate with older devices.

This ensures that your Wi-Fi network can accommodate a variety of devices, from the latest smartphones to legacy gadgets.

Picture it as bridging the generation gap, allowing everyone to join the wireless conversation.

Moreover, the evolution of Wi-Fi standards reflects the relentless pursuit of faster speeds, greater capacity, and enhanced reliability.

Think of it as a continuous quest to meet the growing demands of modern connectivity.

The shift from 2.4 GHz to 5 GHz frequencies opened up new possibilities, reducing interference and congestion.

Imagine it as moving from a crowded marketplace to a serene park, where signals flow freely.

The introduction of technologies like MIMO and beamforming improved coverage and signal strength.

Consider it as enhancing the reach and clarity of your wireless conversations.

Wi-Fi 6, in particular, stands as a testament to the relentless innovation in wireless technology.

Picture it as a symphony of speed, efficiency, and reliability orchestrated for today's connected world.

Each chapter in the evolution of Wi-Fi standards represents a significant milestone in the journey of wireless communication.

Think of it as a series of upgrades that continually enhance our ability to stay connected and communicate seamlessly.

Ultimately, understanding these standards is like reading a captivating book—a narrative of progress, innovation, and the promise of a wireless future that continues to unfold before our eyes.

Chapter 3: Advanced Reconnaissance and Target Identification

Delving into the world of in-depth target profiling techniques is like peeling back the layers of a complex puzzle, revealing a wealth of information and insights.

Imagine it as a journey where you become a digital detective, uncovering valuable details about your target.

In this chapter, we'll explore the art of understanding your target on a profound level, equipping you with the knowledge to conduct effective penetration tests and security assessments.

Think of target profiling as the foundation of any successful ethical hacking endeavor—it's the process of gathering, analyzing, and synthesizing information about your target, whether it's an organization, network, or individual.

Consider it as assembling the pieces of a jigsaw puzzle to form a complete picture.

The first step in this process is reconnaissance, which involves collecting data about your target without directly engaging with it.

Picture it as discreetly observing your subject from a distance, learning about their habits and routines.

Open-source intelligence (OSINT) is a valuable tool in this phase, providing access to publicly available information such as websites, social media profiles, and news articles.

Imagine it as scanning the surface to discover the visible pieces of the puzzle.

Social engineering plays a crucial role in target profiling, as it can provide you with valuable insights through human interaction.

Think of it as striking up a conversation with your subject, gaining their trust, and learning about their vulnerabilities. Phishing campaigns, pretexting, and other social engineering techniques can reveal critical information that may be otherwise inaccessible.

Consider it as engaging in a friendly conversation to extract hidden details.

Understanding the technology stack of your target is essential, akin to knowing the tools and equipment your subject uses in daily life.

Imagine it as studying the devices, software, and systems in your target's environment.

This knowledge can help you identify potential vulnerabilities and attack vectors specific to their setup.

Enumeration is another critical phase in target profiling, where you actively seek to discover and catalog information about your target's systems, services, and resources.

Picture it as exploring the rooms of a building to find what's inside.

Scanning techniques, such as port scanning and service fingerprinting, allow you to create a comprehensive inventory of your target's assets.

Vulnerability scanning is a natural extension of enumeration, where you search for weaknesses or security flaws in the target's infrastructure.

Think of it as inspecting the rooms you've discovered for unlocked doors and windows.

Using vulnerability scanning tools and techniques, you can identify potential entry points for exploitation.

Exploitation is the phase where you capitalize on the vulnerabilities you've discovered.

Consider it as opening those unlocked doors and windows to gain access to your target's systems.

This step requires a deep understanding of the target's environment and the specific vulnerabilities you've identified.

Post-exploitation is equally important, as it involves maintaining access and pivoting within the target's network.

Imagine it as navigating through the rooms you've entered, looking for hidden passages and secrets.

Maintaining persistence and covering your tracks are essential aspects of post-exploitation, ensuring that you can continue your assessment undetected.

Think of it as leaving no trace behind and ensuring that the puzzle pieces remain in your hands.

Throughout this process, documentation is your ally, serving as a record of your actions, findings, and progress.

Consider it as creating a detailed map of your journey through the target's landscape.

Detailed documentation is essential not only for your own reference but also for reporting to your client or organization.

In summary, in-depth target profiling techniques are like the tools and skills of a digital detective.

Imagine it as becoming a Sherlock Holmes of the digital realm, uncovering the mysteries of your target with precision and finesse.

By mastering the art of reconnaissance, social engineering, enumeration, vulnerability scanning, exploitation, and post-exploitation, you'll become a proficient ethical hacker capable of conducting thorough security assessments.

Think of it as honing your detective skills, always ready to unravel the secrets and vulnerabilities that lie within the digital world.

As you continue your journey into the world of ethical hacking, remember that responsible and ethical conduct is paramount.

Consider it as upholding the values of trust, integrity, and professionalism in your pursuit of knowledge and security.

With these in-depth target profiling techniques in your arsenal, you'll be well-equipped to navigate the intricate web of cybersecurity and protect the digital landscape from potential threats and vulnerabilities.

Advanced network mapping and enumeration techniques open up a world of possibilities for ethical hackers and security professionals.

Imagine it as acquiring the skills to create a detailed blueprint of a target's network infrastructure, allowing you to identify potential weaknesses and vulnerabilities.

In this chapter, we'll embark on a journey to explore the intricacies of network mapping and enumeration, equipping you with the knowledge to conduct comprehensive security assessments.

Think of network mapping as the art of creating a visual representation of a target's network.

Picture it as sketching a map that reveals the layout of rooms, hallways, and hidden passages in a building.

Mapping enables you to understand the structure of the network, including the location of devices, servers, routers, and switches.

Imagine it as seeing the entire building from a bird's-eye view, with each device as a unique room.

The process begins with passive reconnaissance, where you gather information about the target's network without actively probing it.

Consider it as observing the building's exterior, noting its architecture and entrances.

Passive reconnaissance often involves using open-source intelligence (OSINT) to gather data from publicly available sources.

Think of it as collecting information from sources like websites, social media, and public records.

This phase helps you gather initial data about the target, such as IP addresses, domain names, and email addresses associated with the network.

Picture it as discovering the names and addresses of the building's occupants.

Once you've collected this information, the next step is active reconnaissance, which involves actively probing the target's network to gather more details.

Imagine it as entering the building and exploring each room, noting the layout and contents.

Active reconnaissance techniques include network scanning, which allows you to discover live hosts, open ports, and services running on those hosts.

Think of it as knocking on each room's door to see who's inside and what they're doing.

Port scanning is a critical component of active reconnaissance, helping you identify which services are running on each host.

Consider it as finding out what activities are happening in each room.

Enumeration is the next phase in this process, akin to collecting valuable information about the devices and services discovered during scanning.

Picture it as cataloging the objects and activities in each room of the building.

Enumeration techniques involve querying services to retrieve specific information, such as user accounts, shares, and system details.

Imagine it as striking up conversations with the occupants of each room to learn more about them.

Common enumeration methods include SNMP (Simple Network Management Protocol) enumeration, which provides insights into network devices, and LDAP (Lightweight Directory Access Protocol) enumeration, which reveals user and group information.

Think of SNMP as asking the building's management about its infrastructure and LDAP as inquiring about the residents.

DNS (Domain Name System) enumeration is another valuable technique, helping you identify hosts associated with the target's domain.

Consider it as learning the names of the occupants in each room.

Service enumeration involves querying services to gather information about their configurations and vulnerabilities.

Picture it as asking the occupants about their interests and hobbies.

Advanced enumeration techniques, such as banner grabbing and version detection, allow you to obtain specific details about services' versions and potential weaknesses.

Imagine it as getting to know the occupants' preferences and vulnerabilities.

Enumeration is a meticulous process that requires patience and attention to detail, as it forms the foundation for subsequent phases of the security assessment.

Think of it as collecting puzzle pieces that will eventually reveal the bigger picture.

Throughout this journey, documentation plays a crucial role, serving as a record of your findings, methods, and progress.

Consider it as creating a detailed journal of your exploration, complete with maps and notes.

Comprehensive documentation not only aids in understanding the target's network but also facilitates reporting to your client or organization.

Picture it as presenting your findings and discoveries in a clear and organized manner.

In summary, advanced network mapping and enumeration techniques are like the tools and skills of a master detective.

Imagine it as becoming a Sherlock Holmes of the digital realm, uncovering the intricacies of a target's network with precision and finesse.

By mastering the art of passive and active reconnaissance, port scanning, enumeration, and documentation, you'll become a proficient ethical hacker capable of conducting thorough security assessments.

Think of it as honing your detective skills, always ready to uncover the secrets and vulnerabilities hidden within the digital landscape.

As you continue your journey into the world of ethical hacking, remember the importance of responsible and ethical conduct.

Consider it as upholding the values of trust, integrity, and professionalism in your pursuit of knowledge and security. With advanced network mapping and enumeration techniques at your disposal, you'll be well-prepared to navigate the complex terrain of cybersecurity and uncover the insights needed to protect digital landscapes from potential threats and vulnerabilities.

Chapter 4: Exploiting Wireless Network Misconfigurations

Identifying and exploiting common misconfigurations is a crucial aspect of ethical hacking and security assessments. Think of it as uncovering unlocked doors and windows in a building's security, allowing you to gain unauthorized access.

In this chapter, we'll explore the art of recognizing and capitalizing on misconfigurations, equipping you with the skills to strengthen security by identifying and rectifying these issues.

Misconfigurations occur when systems, networks, or applications are not set up properly, leaving them vulnerable to exploitation.

Imagine it as a building with doors left ajar, offering an open invitation to intruders.

These errors can result from human mistakes, lack of expertise, or rushed implementations.

Picture it as someone failing to lock the doors or windows before leaving.

One common misconfiguration is weak or default passwords, where users or administrators fail to set strong, unique passwords.

Think of it as leaving the front door unlocked with a "welcome" sign for attackers.

Exploiting weak passwords can provide attackers with easy access to systems and accounts.

Consider it as intruders effortlessly entering the building.

Default configurations, often used by manufacturers for convenience, can be another security pitfall.

Imagine it as using a standard lock on every door in a neighborhood.

Attackers can exploit these defaults, as many users neglect to change them.

Picture it as burglars using a universal key to enter multiple homes.

Another misconfiguration involves unnecessary open ports and services.

Think of it as having too many entry points into the building.

Services that are not needed should be disabled to reduce the attack surface.

Consider it as closing unnecessary doors and windows to enhance security.

Improper file permissions are yet another common misconfiguration.

Imagine it as leaving sensitive documents lying around in plain view.

When users have excessive access privileges, it can lead to data leaks and unauthorized access.

Picture it as allowing anyone to enter any room in the building.

Misconfigured firewalls and access control lists (ACLs) can leave networks vulnerable.

Think of it as having a security guard who doesn't check credentials.

These security measures should be correctly set up to filter traffic effectively.

Consider it as ensuring that only authorized individuals can enter the building.

Outdated software and unpatched systems are a goldmine for attackers.

Imagine it as leaving the building's security system in disrepair.

Exploiting known vulnerabilities in outdated software is a common tactic.

Picture it as criminals exploiting known weaknesses in the security system.

One misconfiguration that often goes unnoticed is excessive information leakage.

Think of it as disclosing sensitive information on social media.

Applications and websites should avoid revealing unnecessary details that could aid attackers.

Consider it as keeping personal information private to prevent intrusions.

Inadequate logging and monitoring can hinder incident detection.

Imagine it as having no security cameras to record suspicious activities.

Without proper monitoring, misconfigurations may remain undetected until a security breach occurs.

Picture it as a break-in going unnoticed until valuables are stolen.

When it comes to exploiting misconfigurations, attackers often follow a systematic approach.

Think of it as methodically checking every door and window for vulnerabilities.

Enumeration, the process of gathering information about the target, is the first step.

Consider it as scouting the building to identify potential weaknesses.

Tools like Nmap, which can identify open ports and services, are commonly used.

Imagine it as using specialized tools to probe for vulnerabilities.

Once vulnerabilities are identified, attackers attempt to exploit them.

Think of it as intruders attempting to pick locks or exploit known weaknesses.

Exploits can be in the form of code, scripts, or other attack vectors.

Consider it as burglars using tools to gain unauthorized access.

Post-exploitation is the final phase, where attackers maintain access and potentially escalate privileges.

Imagine it as intruders exploring the building, looking for hidden treasures.

For ethical hackers, the goal is not to exploit misconfigurations for malicious purposes but to identify them and help organizations strengthen their security.

Picture it as a security consultant providing recommendations to fortify the building's defenses.

Penetration testers and security professionals use the same techniques as attackers to uncover misconfigurations.

Think of it as hiring a locksmith to test the building's security.

Their findings are then used to remediate vulnerabilities and enhance security.

Consider it as reinforcing doors, windows, and security measures to prevent unauthorized access.

In summary, identifying and exploiting common misconfigurations is a critical skill for ethical hackers and security professionals.

Imagine it as providing an essential service to strengthen the security of digital landscapes.

By understanding the types of misconfigurations and following a systematic approach to exploit them, you can help organizations safeguard their systems and networks from potential threats.

Think of it as playing a vital role in maintaining the integrity and confidentiality of digital assets.

As you continue your journey into the world of ethical hacking, always remember the importance of responsible and ethical conduct.

Consider it as upholding the values of trust, integrity, and professionalism in your pursuit of knowledge and security.

With the knowledge and skills to identify and remediate misconfigurations, you'll be well-prepared to navigate the complex terrain of cybersecurity and contribute to a safer digital environment.

Escalating privileges in misconfigured networks is a crucial aspect of ethical hacking and security assessments. It involves taking advantage of weaknesses in network configurations to gain elevated access rights. Think of it as finding a hidden key that unlocks additional doors within a building's security system. In this chapter, we'll delve into the art of privilege escalation, equipping you with the skills to understand, identify, and exploit misconfigurations that lead to elevated privileges.

Misconfigurations, as we discussed earlier, can create opportunities for attackers. When it comes to privilege escalation, these misconfigurations often revolve around user permissions, access controls, and vulnerabilities in the operating system or applications. Imagine it as discovering a master key that grants access to restricted areas of a building.

One common privilege escalation scenario involves unpatched vulnerabilities in the operating system or software. Vulnerabilities are like cracks in a wall that can be exploited to break through. Attackers search for these vulnerabilities and leverage them to gain higher privileges. Picture it as using a crowbar to pry open a locked door.

Another avenue for privilege escalation is misconfigured user accounts and permissions. Imagine it as having keys that open more doors than they should. When users have excessive access rights, it becomes possible to access sensitive data or execute critical commands. Attackers exploit this by impersonating legitimate users or abusing their privileges.

Consider it as someone pretending to be an authorized employee to gain access to secure areas. In this case, it's the digital equivalent. The misconfiguration lies in granting too much trust to users.

Weak authentication mechanisms, such as simple passwords or lack of two-factor authentication, can also lead to privilege escalation. Think of it as having a weak lock on a door. Attackers can crack weak passwords or steal credentials to gain unauthorized access, and once inside, they may escalate their privileges.

Inadequate logging and monitoring are often companions to privilege escalation. It's like attempting a break-in without anyone noticing. Without proper monitoring, attackers can execute privilege escalation attacks without leaving a trace. Effective logging and monitoring are crucial for early detection and response.

Privilege escalation is a multi-step process that often begins with initial access to a system or network. Attackers aim to establish a foothold, which can be achieved through various means like exploiting vulnerabilities, gaining access to a low-privileged user account, or using social engineering.

Once inside, they conduct reconnaissance to identify potential targets and assess the existing privileges. Think of it as intruders exploring a building, looking for valuable items to steal. Attackers search for misconfigurations that could be exploited to elevate their privileges.

Enumeration, the process of gathering information about the system or network, plays a pivotal role. It's like spies gathering intelligence before a mission. Enumeration techniques include examining file permissions, checking for software vulnerabilities, and identifying weak passwords.

Exploitation is the next step, where attackers use the information gathered during enumeration to exploit misconfigurations or vulnerabilities. They may execute code, manipulate user accounts, or escalate privileges through various methods, such as privilege escalation exploits, privilege escalation through social engineering, or privilege escalation through lateral movement.

Privilege escalation exploits target specific vulnerabilities that allow attackers to elevate their privileges. It's akin to finding a secret passage that leads to a higher level of access within the building.

Social engineering in privilege escalation involves manipulating individuals to divulge sensitive information or perform actions that aid the attacker in gaining higher privileges. Think of it as convincing someone to hand over their key to restricted areas.

Lateral movement is the process of moving horizontally across a network to gain access to other systems and escalate privileges further. Picture it as intruders using hidden passages to move from room to room within a building, each time gaining more access.

Post-exploitation is the final stage, where attackers consolidate their control over the compromised system or network. They may install backdoors, create additional user accounts, or modify configurations to maintain access even if the initial entry point is discovered and closed.

In ethical hacking and penetration testing, privilege escalation is a critical phase. It helps organizations understand the vulnerabilities in their systems and how an attacker could potentially escalate their privileges. By simulating these attacks, security professionals can recommend and implement necessary security measures to prevent such escalations.

Consider it as a security consultant helping the building's owner fortify weak points in the security system.

In summary, privilege escalation in misconfigured networks is a complex but essential topic in the realm of ethical hacking and security. Understanding the vulnerabilities that lead to elevated privileges and the methods used by attackers is crucial for securing digital environments.

By learning to recognize and exploit misconfigurations, ethical hackers play a vital role in enhancing the security posture of organizations. They help ensure that unauthorized access is prevented, sensitive data is protected, and potential threats are identified and addressed proactively.

As you continue your journey into the world of ethical hacking, remember that with great knowledge comes great responsibility. Your skills and expertise are valuable assets in the ongoing battle to safeguard digital assets and maintain the trust of individuals and organizations in the digital age.

Chapter 5: Intricate Wireless Encryption Bypass Techniques

Encryption algorithms, which are the backbone of data security, play a crucial role in safeguarding sensitive information in the digital world. However, as technology advances, so do the techniques and methods employed by malicious actors to break encryption and gain unauthorized access to protected data. In this chapter, we will explore advanced attacks against encryption algorithms, shedding light on the evolving landscape of encryption vulnerabilities and the tools and strategies used to exploit them.

Encryption, in its essence, is the process of converting plain text or data into a scrambled format, making it unreadable without the appropriate decryption key. It serves as a shield against eavesdropping and unauthorized access, ensuring the confidentiality and integrity of sensitive information.

As encryption algorithms become more sophisticated and robust, attackers are forced to develop advanced techniques to bypass these security measures. Imagine encryption as a formidable fortress protecting a treasure, and attackers as cunning thieves devising ingenious ways to breach its defenses.

One of the most common advanced attacks against encryption is known as brute-force attacks. In this method, attackers attempt to decrypt encrypted data by systematically trying every possible key until the correct one is found. Picture it as an intruder tirelessly testing every key in a vast keyring until they find the one that unlocks the treasure chest.

Brute-force attacks can be time-consuming and resource-intensive, especially when dealing with strong encryption algorithms and long encryption keys. However, attackers employ specialized hardware, parallel processing, and distributed computing to accelerate the decryption process.

Another formidable adversary of encryption is the chosen plaintext attack. In this scenario, attackers gain access to both the encrypted text and its corresponding plaintext, allowing them to analyze the encryption algorithm's behavior and deduce the encryption key. Think of it as observing a locksmith open a lock and then replicating the process to unlock similar locks.

Chosen plaintext attacks are particularly insidious because they exploit vulnerabilities in the encryption process itself. To mitigate this threat, encryption algorithms must be designed with resistance against chosen plaintext attacks in mind.

Side-channel attacks represent yet another sophisticated approach to breaking encryption. Instead of targeting the encryption algorithm directly, these attacks focus on the physical or electromagnetic emanations, power consumption, or timing characteristics of the encryption process. It's akin to listening for subtle sounds or vibrations while someone is attempting to unlock a door.

For example, a timing attack observes the time it takes for an encryption algorithm to process data and uses this information to deduce the encryption key. By meticulously measuring the time differences, attackers can infer crucial details about the encryption process.

Cache-based attacks, on the other hand, exploit the behavior of a computer's cache memory during encryption and decryption. Attackers can deduce sensitive information by monitoring cache hits and misses, revealing key details about the encryption process.

Quantum computing introduces a new dimension to the encryption battle. Quantum computers leverage the principles of quantum mechanics, enabling them to perform calculations at speeds that far surpass classical computers. While this promises breakthroughs in various fields, it also poses a significant threat to traditional encryption algorithms.

Quantum computers are theoretically capable of efficiently solving complex mathematical problems that underpin many encryption techniques, such as factoring large numbers. As a result, they have the potential to break widely used encryption schemes, like RSA and ECC, rendering existing cryptographic systems obsolete.

To counter the impending threat of quantum computing, researchers are developing post-quantum cryptography, which focuses on encryption algorithms resistant to quantum attacks. These emerging encryption techniques aim to secure data against the computational power of quantum computers.

In addition to these advanced attacks, attackers continuously explore various methods, such as zero-day exploits, compromised encryption keys, and insider threats, to compromise encrypted data. Zero-day exploits target previously unknown vulnerabilities in encryption software or hardware, providing attackers with the element of surprise.

Compromised encryption keys can be obtained through various means, including social engineering, insider collusion, or even sophisticated espionage. Once in possession of the encryption keys, attackers can decrypt sensitive data with ease, bypassing the encryption's protective layer.

Insider threats pose a unique challenge as they involve individuals within an organization who misuse their access privileges to compromise data security intentionally. These threats may involve employees with legitimate access to encryption keys and confidential information, making them difficult to detect.

The evolving landscape of advanced attacks against encryption emphasizes the need for continuous research, innovation, and proactive security measures. Encryption remains a fundamental pillar of cybersecurity, but its effectiveness relies on staying ahead of the curve in understanding and countering emerging threats.

In the ongoing battle between those who seek to protect sensitive information and those who seek to exploit it, the outcome depends on the vigilance, adaptability, and commitment of security professionals, researchers, and organizations worldwide.

As technology advances, encryption algorithms will continue to evolve, becoming more resilient against advanced attacks. The collaboration between experts in the field, the development of post-quantum cryptography, and the adoption of best practices in encryption implementation are essential steps toward securing the digital world against the ever-present threats to data privacy and security.

In this fast-paced digital age, encryption stands as a beacon of hope, ensuring that sensitive data remains confidential and secure. It is a testament to human ingenuity in the face of evolving threats, a digital fortress that must withstand the relentless assaults of the cyber realm.

As we delve deeper into the realm of advanced attacks against encryption algorithms, remember that knowledge is your most potent weapon in the fight against cyber threats. Stay informed, stay vigilant, and stay committed to the principles of data security. Your role in protecting the digital world is more critical than ever.

Decrypting Wi-Fi traffic and capturing sensitive data represents a critical aspect of network penetration testing and ethical hacking. In this chapter, we'll delve into the techniques and tools used to intercept, decrypt, and analyze Wi-Fi traffic for the purpose of evaluating network security.

Wi-Fi networks are ubiquitous in our modern world, providing convenient access to the internet and local resources. However, the convenience of Wi-Fi comes with potential security risks, as wireless communication is susceptible to eavesdropping and interception. To assess the vulnerability of a Wi-Fi network, ethical hackers employ decryption techniques that mirror the methods employed by malicious actors, but with a legitimate and constructive purpose.

One of the primary goals of decrypting Wi-Fi traffic is to gain insight into the data being transmitted over the network. This data can include sensitive information such as login credentials, financial transactions, personal messages, and more. By decrypting and capturing this data, security professionals can evaluate the effectiveness of encryption protocols and the overall security posture of the network.

Wi-Fi traffic interception often begins with the deployment of a packet sniffer or network analyzer. These tools passively monitor the wireless network, capturing data packets as they are transmitted between devices. Think of it as listening in on a conversation between two people without their knowledge.

To effectively decrypt Wi-Fi traffic, ethical hackers must first identify the encryption method employed by the network. The most common encryption standards are WEP (Wired Equivalent Privacy), WPA (Wi-Fi Protected Access), and WPA2/WPA3. Each of these standards presents different levels of security and complexity in terms of decryption.

WEP, for example, is notoriously weak and can be cracked relatively easily using readily available tools. Ethical hackers may use techniques like the Fluhrer-Mantin-Shamir (FMS) attack or the Chop-Chop attack to recover WEP encryption keys. It's akin to picking a lock with a known vulnerability.

WPA and WPA2/WPA3, on the other hand, are more robust encryption methods. Decrypting traffic protected by these standards typically involves capturing a WPA handshake, which occurs when a device connects to the network. Ethical hackers use techniques like deauthentication attacks to force devices to reconnect and capture the handshake.

Once the WPA handshake is obtained, ethical hackers can employ brute-force attacks or dictionary attacks to crack the Wi-Fi password and gain access to the encryption key. These attacks involve systematically testing a list of potential passwords until the correct one is found, similar to trying different keys on a lock until it turns.

In some cases, if the Wi-Fi network uses weak or commonly used passwords, the decryption process can be relatively quick. However, strong and complex passwords can significantly impede these efforts, making it challenging to crack the encryption key.

Decryption tools and techniques continue to evolve, and some attackers may employ advanced methods, including the use of rainbow tables, which are precomputed tables of hashed passwords, to expedite the password cracking process. The arms race between encryption and decryption techniques is an ongoing battle in the realm of Wi-Fi security.

It's worth noting that ethical hackers perform these activities within the bounds of legality and ethical guidelines. They have the explicit consent of network owners or organizations to conduct penetration tests and security assessments. Unauthorized interception and decryption of Wi-Fi traffic are illegal and unethical.

Decrypting Wi-Fi traffic is not solely about breaking encryption; it also involves analyzing the data packets for vulnerabilities and security weaknesses. Ethical hackers scrutinize the network for misconfigurations, outdated encryption protocols, or insecure practices that could expose sensitive data to potential attackers.

Additionally, ethical hackers often utilize tools like Wireshark, a widely-used packet analysis software, to inspect captured data packets. Wireshark allows them to examine the content of the traffic, identify potential security issues, and provide recommendations for improving network security.

In summary, decrypting Wi-Fi traffic is a crucial aspect of network penetration testing and ethical hacking. It enables security professionals to assess the effectiveness of encryption methods, identify vulnerabilities, and provide recommendations for enhancing network security. As technology evolves, so do the tools and techniques used in decryption, making it an ongoing and dynamic field within the realm of cybersecurity

Chapter 6: Advanced Denial-of-Service (DoS) Attacks

Sophisticated Denial of Service (DoS) attack vectors represent a significant threat to network and system availability in today's digital landscape. In this chapter, we will explore the intricacies of these advanced attack techniques, shedding light on their potential impact and the strategies to mitigate them.

DoS attacks have been a persistent threat to online services and networks for many years. They aim to disrupt the normal functioning of a system or network by overwhelming it with a flood of traffic, causing it to become unresponsive to legitimate users. While traditional DoS attacks are well-known and often relatively straightforward, sophisticated DoS attack vectors take these disruptions to a new level of complexity and effectiveness.

One such sophisticated DoS attack vector is the Distributed Denial of Service (DDoS) attack. Unlike a traditional DoS attack, where a single source generates traffic to overwhelm a target, DDoS attacks involve multiple compromised devices, often forming a botnet, launching coordinated attacks. These attacks are challenging to defend against because they can originate from thousands or even millions of different IP addresses, making it difficult to identify and block the malicious traffic.

Within the realm of DDoS attacks, several variants exist, each with unique characteristics. One such variant is the amplification attack, where attackers use vulnerable servers to amplify their attack traffic, making it more potent. DNS amplification and NTP amplification are examples of this technique. By exploiting poorly configured servers, attackers can significantly increase the volume of traffic directed at the target.

Another sophisticated DDoS vector is the application layer attack, often referred to as an HTTP flood or Layer 7 attack. These attacks target specific web applications, attempting to overwhelm them with a barrage of seemingly legitimate HTTP requests. Unlike traditional DDoS attacks that focus on network-level disruption, application layer attacks seek to exhaust server resources by targeting the application itself, making them particularly challenging to mitigate.

Beyond DDoS attacks, attackers may employ techniques like resource depletion attacks. These attacks aim to exhaust specific resources within a target system or network. For instance, a slowloris attack targets web servers by initiating numerous partial HTTP requests, tying up the server's available connections and rendering it unresponsive to legitimate users.

Another sophisticated DoS attack vector is the protocol-based attack, which leverages vulnerabilities or weaknesses in network protocols. For example, a SYN flood attack targets the TCP handshake process by sending a high volume of TCP SYN packets, exhausting the server's resources and preventing legitimate connections.

Advanced DoS attacks can also employ reflective techniques, where attackers bounce their traffic off third-party servers to obscure the source of the attack. These reflection attacks can be challenging to trace back to their origin, complicating the mitigation process.

To mitigate the impact of sophisticated DoS attacks, organizations must adopt a multi-faceted approach to defense. This includes network-level protections such as rate limiting, traffic filtering, and the use of intrusion prevention systems (IPS) to detect and block malicious traffic. Content delivery networks (CDNs) can also help distribute traffic and absorb the impact of DDoS attacks.

Application-level protections are equally important. Web application firewalls (WAFs) can help filter out malicious HTTP requests, while load balancing and redundant systems can distribute traffic and ensure service availability during an attack.

Intrusion detection systems (IDS) and intrusion prevention systems (IPS) play a critical role in identifying and mitigating sophisticated DoS attacks. These systems monitor network traffic for unusual patterns and can automatically take action to block or mitigate malicious traffic.

Additionally, organizations should have an incident response plan in place, enabling them to respond swiftly and effectively to DoS attacks when they occur. Regular testing and simulation exercises can help ensure that teams are well-prepared to handle such incidents.

In summary, sophisticated DoS attack vectors represent a formidable challenge in the realm of cybersecurity. These advanced techniques, including DDoS attacks, application layer attacks, resource depletion attacks, and protocol-based attacks, pose a significant threat to the availability of online services and networks. To defend against these threats, organizations must adopt a multi-layered approach to security, encompassing network-level protections, application-level defenses, and robust incident response plans. Staying vigilant and proactive in the face of evolving attack methods is essential to maintaining a resilient digital infrastructure.

Mitigation and defense against advanced Denial of Service (DoS) attacks are crucial aspects of modern cybersecurity practices. In this chapter, we will explore various strategies and techniques to protect networks, systems, and applications from the evolving landscape of sophisticated DoS threats.

As we've discussed in previous chapters, advanced DoS attacks, such as Distributed Denial of Service (DDoS) attacks and application layer attacks, pose significant challenges to organizations. To effectively mitigate and defend against these threats, organizations must adopt a proactive and multi-layered approach to security.

One fundamental strategy for mitigating DDoS attacks is network traffic filtering. This involves the use of firewalls, intrusion prevention systems (IPS), and rate limiting to identify and block malicious traffic before it reaches the target network or application. By configuring these defenses to recognize and filter out anomalous traffic patterns, organizations can significantly reduce the impact of DDoS attacks.

Content Delivery Networks (CDNs) also play a vital role in defending against DDoS attacks. CDNs are designed to distribute traffic across multiple servers and data centers, ensuring that the network can absorb large volumes of incoming requests. This distributed architecture can help mitigate the effects of volumetric DDoS attacks by preventing them from overwhelming a single point of entry.

Another effective DDoS mitigation strategy is the use of traffic scrubbing services. These services work by diverting incoming traffic through a scrubbing center, where it is analyzed and filtered to remove malicious traffic. The clean traffic is then forwarded to the target network or application. This approach helps ensure that only legitimate traffic reaches the intended destination.

Application layer attacks, which target specific web applications or services, require specialized mitigation techniques. Web Application Firewalls (WAFs) are designed to filter out malicious HTTP requests and protect against SQL injection, cross-site scripting (XSS), and other application layer vulnerabilities. WAFs are essential for safeguarding web-based services from sophisticated attacks that aim to exhaust server resources or compromise data integrity.

Load balancing and redundancy are critical components of DDoS defense. By distributing incoming traffic across multiple servers or data centers, organizations can ensure that no single point of failure exists. This approach not only enhances availability but also makes it more challenging for attackers to pinpoint vulnerable targets.

Intrusion Detection Systems (IDS) and Intrusion Prevention Systems (IPS) are valuable tools for identifying and mitigating DDoS attacks in real-time. These systems analyze network traffic patterns and can automatically take action to block or throttle malicious traffic, reducing the impact of the attack.

While technical defenses are crucial, organizations must also have robust incident response plans in place. These plans outline the steps to be taken when a DoS attack occurs, including communication strategies, incident analysis, and mitigation procedures. Regular training and simulation exercises can help ensure that response teams are well-prepared to handle DoS incidents effectively.

Additionally, organizations should consider implementing rate limiting and rate shaping to control the flow of incoming traffic. By setting limits on the number of requests or connections that can be established within a certain time frame, organizations can reduce the risk of resource exhaustion and application layer attacks.

It's essential to monitor network and application performance continuously. Anomalies in traffic patterns or unexpected resource utilization can be early indicators of a DoS attack. Effective monitoring can help organizations detect and respond to attacks promptly.

Collaboration with Internet Service Providers (ISPs) is another critical aspect of DDoS defense. Many ISPs offer DDoS mitigation services that can help filter out malicious traffic before it reaches an organization's network. Establishing communication and coordination with ISPs can enhance overall defense capabilities.

Application and system hardening should not be overlooked. Organizations should regularly review and update their configurations, applying security best practices to reduce attack surfaces. This includes patching known vulnerabilities, disabling unnecessary services, and employing strong authentication and access controls.

In summary, mitigation and defense against advanced DoS attacks require a comprehensive and multi-faceted approach to cybersecurity. Organizations must implement network-level protections, application-specific defenses, and robust incident response plans to effectively safeguard against evolving threats. By staying proactive, collaborating with ISPs, and maintaining a strong security posture, organizations can significantly reduce their vulnerability to advanced DoS attacks and ensure the availability and integrity of their digital assets.

Chapter 7: Leveraging Wireless Device Vulnerabilities

Identifying and exploiting device weaknesses is a critical aspect of penetration testing and ethical hacking, aimed at uncovering vulnerabilities in various hardware components and exploiting them to gain unauthorized access or control.

Devices encompass a wide range of equipment, including routers, switches, cameras, IoT devices, and more. Each of these devices may have unique weaknesses that can be identified and leveraged for various purposes, such as network infiltration, data exfiltration, or device manipulation.

One common approach to identifying device weaknesses is through vulnerability scanning and assessment. Penetration testers use specialized tools and techniques to scan the target network for known vulnerabilities in devices and their firmware or software. These assessments can reveal security flaws, unpatched vulnerabilities, or misconfigurations that can be exploited.

Firmware analysis is another essential aspect of device weakness identification. Firmware is the software that runs on hardware devices, and vulnerabilities within it can lead to significant security risks. Penetration testers often analyze firmware to identify vulnerabilities, such as hardcoded passwords, backdoors, or buffer overflows that can be exploited to compromise the device.

Physical device testing is also crucial for identifying weaknesses. In some cases, attackers may have physical access to devices, making it important to assess their physical security. This can include tamper-resistant measures, device seals, or the presence of exposed ports or interfaces that could be exploited.

Device misconfigurations are a common source of weaknesses. Devices are often configured with default settings that may not be secure, such as default passwords or open ports. Penetration testers actively seek these misconfigurations, as they can provide a straightforward path to device exploitation.

Exploiting device weaknesses often involves the use of specialized tools and techniques. For example, if a device has a known vulnerability, an attacker may use an exploit script or tool to take advantage of that weakness. These tools automate the exploitation process and can provide attackers with unauthorized access or control.

Social engineering can also play a role in identifying and exploiting device weaknesses. By posing as legitimate users or technicians, attackers may manipulate device owners or operators into revealing sensitive information, such as login credentials or access codes, that can be used to compromise the device.

Once device weaknesses are identified, it's essential to assess the potential impact of their exploitation. This involves understanding the context in which the device operates and the potential consequences of a successful attack. For example, compromising a security camera may allow an attacker to gain access to sensitive video footage or even manipulate the camera to hide their activities.

In addition to assessing the impact, penetration testers must consider the legal and ethical aspects of exploiting device weaknesses. Ethical hacking involves adhering to a strict code of conduct and legal guidelines. Unauthorized access or exploitation of devices is illegal and can lead to serious consequences.

Therefore, it's crucial for penetration testers to obtain proper authorization and follow ethical hacking practices. This typically involves working under the supervision and permission of the organization responsible for the devices being tested, with clear rules of engagement and boundaries in place.

Device weaknesses can vary widely, and their exploitation can have different goals. Some attackers may seek financial gain, while others may aim to disrupt operations or compromise sensitive data. Identifying and exploiting these weaknesses is a key part of penetration testing, helping organizations strengthen their security measures and protect against potential threats.

Overall, the process of identifying and exploiting device weaknesses requires a combination of technical expertise, ethical considerations, and a thorough understanding of the target environment. It is a vital component of ethical hacking and cybersecurity efforts, helping organizations proactively address vulnerabilities and enhance their overall security posture.

Gaining control over compromised devices is a critical phase in the realm of ethical hacking and penetration testing, as it allows security professionals to assess the extent of a security breach and mitigate potential risks. When a device is compromised, it means that an attacker has successfully infiltrated it and gained unauthorized access or control. This can happen due to various vulnerabilities, including software flaws, misconfigurations, or the exploitation of weaknesses.

The process of gaining control over compromised devices typically begins with the initial breach. Once an attacker has identified a vulnerability and exploited it, they may gain a foothold on the compromised device. This initial access point can provide them with limited control and visibility within the target system.

Once inside the compromised device, the attacker's goal is often to escalate their privileges. Privilege escalation involves gaining higher levels of access and control within the system, allowing the attacker to perform more advanced actions and potentially take over the device completely.

Privilege escalation can take various forms, depending on the specific vulnerabilities and weaknesses present. It may involve exploiting known vulnerabilities in the device's operating system or software to gain administrative or root-level access. Alternatively, attackers may use techniques like privilege escalation exploits, privilege escalation scripts, or even social engineering to trick users or administrators into granting higher privileges.

One common method for privilege escalation is the use of malware or malicious code. Attackers may deploy malware on the compromised device, which can then be used to escalate privileges and maintain persistence. Malware can include Trojans, rootkits, backdoors, or other types of malicious software that allow attackers to maintain control even after the initial breach is discovered and mitigated.

Persistence is a crucial aspect of gaining control over compromised devices. Attackers aim to maintain access to the compromised device for as long as possible, ensuring that they can continue to gather information, carry out attacks, or use the device as a pivot point for further attacks within the network. Achieving persistence often involves establishing mechanisms that allow the attacker to regain access even after the device has been rebooted or security measures have been implemented.

Common techniques for achieving persistence include the creation of hidden or persistent backdoors, the modification of startup scripts or scheduled tasks, or the manipulation of system settings to maintain access. These techniques are designed to evade detection and enable the attacker to retain control over the compromised device over an extended period.

Another aspect of gaining control over compromised devices is data exfiltration. Attackers often seek to extract sensitive information or data from the compromised device for their own purposes, such as stealing intellectual property, financial data, or personal information. Data exfiltration techniques can vary, ranging from simple file transfers to more sophisticated methods that disguise the traffic to avoid detection.

Gaining control over compromised devices is a complex and multi-faceted process, requiring in-depth knowledge of security vulnerabilities, operating systems, and network protocols. It also demands a deep understanding of ethical considerations, as penetration testers must adhere to strict ethical guidelines and legal boundaries when attempting to gain control over compromised devices.

Moreover, gaining control over compromised devices highlights the importance of proactive security measures to prevent initial compromises. Organizations should focus on practices such as regular patching and updates, robust access controls, intrusion detection systems, and network segmentation to reduce the risk of device compromise.

In summary, gaining control over compromised devices is a pivotal phase in ethical hacking and penetration testing, allowing security professionals to assess vulnerabilities, evaluate the extent of the breach, and strengthen security measures. It underscores the critical need for organizations to prioritize cybersecurity and adopt proactive strategies to defend against potential breaches and unauthorized access to their devices and networks.

Chapter 8: Advanced Wireless Post-Exploitation Techniques

Privilege escalation and lateral movement are two critical aspects of ethical hacking and penetration testing within Wi-Fi networks, and they play a pivotal role in assessing and fortifying security measures. These concepts revolve around the idea that, once an attacker gains initial access to a network or device, they seek to expand their influence and control over the system.

Privilege escalation, as the name suggests, involves elevating one's level of access or control within a network or device. In the context of Wi-Fi networks, this typically refers to gaining higher-level privileges that allow the attacker to execute more advanced and impactful actions. The ultimate goal of privilege escalation is to attain administrative or root-level access, which provides the attacker with almost unrestricted control.

Lateral movement, on the other hand, focuses on the horizontal expansion of an attacker's presence within a network. Once an attacker has successfully compromised a single device or user account, they seek to move laterally to other devices or areas of the network. This lateral movement can involve exploiting vulnerabilities, using stolen credentials, or leveraging compromised devices as stepping stones to access more critical assets.

Privilege escalation often precedes lateral movement because it grants the attacker the necessary permissions to move freely within the network. By obtaining higher privileges, the attacker can access additional resources, systems, and data, expanding their reach and potential impact.

There are various techniques and methods used for privilege escalation and lateral movement in Wi-Fi networks. These techniques can be categorized into several common approaches:

Exploiting Vulnerabilities: Attackers may exploit known vulnerabilities in Wi-Fi network components, such as routers, access points, or devices, to gain elevated privileges. This can include leveraging software or firmware flaws, misconfigurations, or weak security settings.

Credential Theft: Stealing login credentials is a prevalent method for privilege escalation. Attackers may use techniques like password cracking, brute-force attacks, or phishing to obtain usernames and passwords, enabling them to access accounts with higher privileges.

Privilege Escalation Exploits: Attackers may use specific exploits or vulnerabilities in the operating system or software of compromised devices to escalate their privileges. This can involve taking advantage of zero-day vulnerabilities or unpatched weaknesses.

Social Engineering: Social engineering techniques can be employed to manipulate individuals into granting higher privileges or disclosing sensitive information. This can include tactics like pretexting, baiting, or tailgating.

Post-Exploitation Tools: Once initial access is gained, attackers often use post-exploitation tools to further their objectives. These tools can help with privilege escalation, lateral movement, and maintaining persistence within the network.

Pivot Points: Compromised devices can serve as pivot points for lateral movement. Attackers can use these devices as proxies to access other segments of the network or launch attacks on neighboring systems.

Pass-the-Hash: This technique involves extracting password hashes from compromised devices and using them to authenticate and gain access to other network resources without knowing the plaintext passwords.

It's essential to highlight that privilege escalation and lateral movement are not exclusive to Wi-Fi networks but apply to network security in general. The successful execution of these tactics relies on the attacker's knowledge of the network's architecture, the target's security posture, and the availability of vulnerabilities.

For ethical hackers and penetration testers, understanding privilege escalation and lateral movement is crucial for assessing network security and identifying potential weaknesses. By simulating these techniques, security professionals can help organizations identify and remediate vulnerabilities, enhancing their overall security posture.

In summary, privilege escalation and lateral movement are integral components of ethical hacking and penetration testing within Wi-Fi networks. These concepts underscore the importance of robust security measures, regular patching and updates, access controls, and user awareness training to mitigate the risk of unauthorized access and movement within networks. As the cybersecurity landscape evolves, staying informed about these techniques is vital for protecting Wi-Fi networks and the sensitive data they carry.

Maintaining persistent access and data exfiltration are critical elements of advanced cyberattacks, and understanding these tactics is essential for both defenders and ethical hackers. These techniques are often employed by sophisticated adversaries seeking to maintain long-term control over compromised systems or steal sensitive information discreetly.

When we talk about maintaining persistent access, we refer to the ability of an attacker to maintain a foothold or backdoor into a compromised system or network even after initial access has been achieved. This persistence allows the attacker to return to the compromised environment at will, without relying on repeated exploitation of vulnerabilities or social engineering tricks.

Persistent access is particularly valuable for attackers because it enables them to maintain control over a compromised system or network, gather more information over time, and potentially expand their influence within the targeted environment. This can have severe consequences, such as data breaches, unauthorized surveillance, or further attacks.

To establish and maintain persistent access, attackers often use various techniques and tools:

Rootkits and Backdoors: Attackers may install rootkits or backdoors on compromised systems. Rootkits are malicious software that hides the presence of the attacker and provides privileged access to the system. Backdoors are typically secret entry points that allow the attacker to bypass normal authentication mechanisms.

Malicious Services: Attackers can create malicious services or scheduled tasks that run automatically on compromised systems. These services can establish a connection with a command and control (C2) server operated by the attacker, providing a channel for remote access and control.

Privilege Escalation: Gaining higher-level privileges within a system or network is essential for maintaining access. Attackers often use privilege escalation techniques to increase their control and visibility within the compromised environment.

Fileless Malware: Fileless malware operates in memory, leaving no traditional traces on disk. Attackers use fileless techniques to evade detection and maintain persistent access by injecting malicious code into legitimate processes.

Data Exfiltration: While maintaining access, attackers may exfiltrate sensitive data from compromised systems. Data can be silently transmitted to remote servers controlled by the attacker, allowing them to steal valuable information over time.

Data exfiltration, on the other hand, involves the unauthorized extraction of data from a compromised system or network. Attackers employ data exfiltration to steal sensitive information, such as intellectual property, financial records, or personally identifiable information (PII). This stolen data can be used for various malicious purposes, including financial gain, espionage, or selling on the dark web.

Data exfiltration techniques vary depending on the attacker's goals and the nature of the compromised environment. Common data exfiltration methods include:

Command and Control (C2) Channels: Attackers establish covert channels to communicate with compromised systems and exfiltrate data. These channels may use encrypted communication protocols, making detection more challenging.

Data Compression and Encryption: Attackers often compress and encrypt stolen data before exfiltration to reduce the volume of transferred data and obfuscate its content.

Steganography: Steganography involves hiding data within seemingly innocuous files or communications. Attackers may embed stolen data within images, documents, or other digital media to avoid detection.

Covert Channels: Attackers can utilize existing network protocols or communication channels in unexpected ways to exfiltrate data without raising suspicion.

Data Splitting: Large volumes of data may be divided into smaller chunks for exfiltration, making it harder to detect abnormal traffic patterns.

Insider Threats: In some cases, insiders with authorized access may misuse their privileges to exfiltrate data. This threat underscores the importance of monitoring and controlling user actions within an organization.

Defending against maintaining persistent access and data exfiltration requires a multi-faceted approach. Organizations should implement robust security measures, such as intrusion detection systems, endpoint protection, and user behavior analytics, to detect and mitigate these threats. Regular security audits and vulnerability assessments can help identify and address vulnerabilities that attackers might exploit to maintain access.

Furthermore, organizations should focus on user awareness and training to recognize and report suspicious activities. Establishing an incident response plan is essential for effectively responding to and mitigating the impact of persistent access and data exfiltration incidents.

In summary, maintaining persistent access and data exfiltration are techniques that adversaries use to maintain control over compromised systems and steal valuable information. Understanding these tactics is crucial for defenders and ethical hackers alike, as it allows them to better protect systems and networks against such threats. By implementing robust security measures, monitoring for suspicious activities, and responding effectively to incidents, organizations can strengthen their cybersecurity posture and mitigate the risks associated with maintaining persistent access and data exfiltration.

Chapter 9: Evading Detection and Covering Tracks

Anti-forensic techniques in Wi-Fi hacking represent a set of strategies and tactics employed by malicious actors to hinder or evade digital forensic investigations, making it challenging for investigators to detect and attribute cyberattacks. These techniques are designed to cover the tracks of attackers, erase or manipulate digital evidence, and complicate the process of tracing the origin of a security breach.

One common anti-forensic approach in Wi-Fi hacking involves the use of anonymization tools and techniques to conceal the true identity and location of the attacker. These tools often include virtual private networks (VPNs), Tor networks, and proxy servers, which route traffic through multiple nodes to obscure the source.

Attackers may also employ IP address spoofing and MAC address spoofing to make it appear as if their activities originate from different locations and devices. This not only confuses investigators but can also lead them on false trails, making it harder to identify the actual attacker.

Data encryption plays a significant role in anti-forensics. Attackers may use strong encryption algorithms to protect their communication and data stored on compromised systems. When properly implemented, encryption can make it extremely difficult for forensic experts to access and analyze data without the decryption keys.

To cover their tracks, attackers often focus on erasing or altering logs and other digital traces of their activities. They may delete event logs, clear browser histories, and remove any evidence of their presence on compromised systems. This makes it challenging for investigators to reconstruct the timeline of an attack and identify the initial entry point.

File wiping and data shredding tools are frequently used to ensure that no remnants of sensitive data or malicious tools remain on compromised systems. These tools overwrite data with random values, making data recovery virtually impossible.

Furthermore, attackers may employ anti-forensic techniques such as steganography, which involves hiding data within other seemingly innocuous files, such as images or documents. This makes it difficult for investigators to detect the presence of hidden information, especially when it is concealed in plain sight.

For instance, an attacker might embed stolen data within a digital image and then transmit it over a compromised Wi-Fi network. To the naked eye, the image appears unchanged, but it contains concealed information that can only be extracted with specialized tools.

Another anti-forensic tactic involves fragmentation and dispersion of digital evidence. Attackers may scatter stolen data across various storage devices, cloud services, or remote servers. This distributed approach makes it harder for investigators to locate and recover all pieces of evidence, especially if the attacker has encrypted or password-protected them.

In some cases, attackers resort to hardware-based anti-forensic techniques. They might use temporary or disposable hardware devices, such as USB drives or Raspberry Pi computers, for their illicit activities. Once the attack is complete, these devices can be easily destroyed or discarded, leaving no physical evidence behind.

Obfuscation and anti-forensic countermeasures continue to evolve alongside advancements in digital forensics. To combat these techniques, digital forensic experts must adapt and develop new methods and tools for evidence collection and analysis. This ongoing cat-and-mouse game highlights the importance of a proactive and comprehensive approach to cybersecurity.

While anti-forensic techniques can pose significant challenges for investigators, they are not foolproof. Skilled forensic experts and cybersecurity professionals are constantly working to improve their capabilities and develop innovative ways to uncover hidden evidence and trace the activities of malicious actors.

In summary, anti-forensic techniques in Wi-Fi hacking are designed to obstruct digital forensic investigations and cover the tracks of attackers. These techniques encompass a wide range of strategies, from anonymization and encryption to data manipulation and file hiding. Despite the challenges they present, the field of digital forensics continues to advance, enabling investigators to uncover and analyze digital evidence even in the face of sophisticated anti-forensic tactics.

In the ever-evolving landscape of cybersecurity, the arms race between attackers and defenders continues to escalate. As cyber threats become more sophisticated, countermeasures for detection and attribution play a pivotal role in identifying, mitigating, and attributing cyberattacks. These measures are critical not only for protecting organizations and individuals but also for holding malicious actors accountable for their actions.

One fundamental aspect of countermeasures for detection and attribution is the implementation of robust intrusion detection systems (IDS) and intrusion prevention systems (IPS). These technologies act as the first line of defense, monitoring network traffic and system activity to identify suspicious or malicious behavior. When anomalies or potential threats are detected, they trigger alerts or automated responses, allowing security teams to investigate and respond promptly.

Behavioral analysis is another key component of detection and attribution. By monitoring the behavior of users, devices, and applications within a network, security professionals can identify deviations from normal patterns. Behavioral analysis can help detect insider threats, zero-day attacks, and advanced persistent threats (APTs) that often employ subtle and evolving tactics to avoid detection.

Machine learning and artificial intelligence (AI) have revolutionized the field of cybersecurity, enhancing the capabilities of detection and attribution. These technologies enable security systems to analyze vast datasets and identify anomalies that may go unnoticed by traditional methods. Machine learning algorithms can adapt and learn from new threats, making them highly effective in identifying previously unseen attack patterns.

Advanced threat intelligence feeds are invaluable resources for detection and attribution. These feeds provide up-to-date information on known threats, malware signatures, and indicators of compromise (IOCs). By integrating threat intelligence into their security infrastructure, organizations can proactively defend against known threats and share information with the broader cybersecurity community to aid in attribution efforts.

Intrusion detection and attribution often involve the collection and analysis of logs and digital footprints left by attackers. Security information and event management (SIEM) systems are indispensable tools for aggregating and correlating log data from various sources. SIEM solutions enable security teams to identify trends, correlate events, and piece together the timeline of an attack, making it easier to attribute malicious activity to specific actors or groups.

Endpoint detection and response (EDR) solutions provide granular visibility into the activities occurring on individual devices within a network. EDR tools can detect malicious processes, file changes, and suspicious network connections, allowing security teams to quickly identify compromised endpoints and take remediation actions.

Packet capture and network forensics play a critical role in attribution efforts. Network traffic analysis can reveal the techniques, tactics, and procedures (TTPs) used by attackers, helping investigators build a comprehensive picture of the attack chain. Packet capture tools record network traffic for later analysis, enabling security experts to reconstruct and analyze the entire attack sequence.

In some cases, threat actors may attempt to hide their tracks by using anonymization techniques, such as VPNs, proxy servers, or Tor networks. Detecting and attributing attacks originating from anonymized sources can be challenging. However, cyber threat intelligence combined with network monitoring can provide valuable insights into the geographical origin and infrastructure used by attackers, aiding in attribution efforts.

Collaboration within the cybersecurity community is essential for effective attribution. Information sharing and collaboration with other organizations, industry groups, and government agencies can help piece together the puzzle of a cyberattack. Sharing threat indicators, attack patterns, and attribution findings can lead to the identification of threat actors and their motives.

International cooperation and diplomacy also play a role in attribution, especially when nation-state actors are involved. Cyberattacks with geopolitical implications require diplomatic efforts to hold responsible parties accountable and deter future malicious activities. Attribution in such cases may involve the use of intelligence agencies, diplomatic channels, and international agreements.

One of the most significant challenges in attribution is the attribution gap—the difficulty of definitively identifying the individuals or entities behind cyberattacks. Attackers often employ deception techniques, false flags, and proxy actors to obfuscate their identity and origin. As a result, attribution may be limited to the attribution of specific tactics, techniques, and infrastructure used in an attack rather than the direct identification of the threat actor.

Legal considerations also come into play in the realm of attribution. To attribute an attack and pursue legal action against threat actors, organizations and law enforcement agencies must gather robust evidence and follow proper legal procedures. The rules and regulations governing cybercrime investigations can vary by jurisdiction and may involve complex international legal frameworks.

In summary, countermeasures for detection and attribution are essential components of modern cybersecurity. These measures encompass a wide range of technologies, practices, and collaboration efforts aimed at identifying, mitigating, and attributing cyberattacks. While attribution challenges persist, advancements in technology, threat intelligence sharing, and international cooperation continue to enhance the capabilities of cybersecurity professionals in their ongoing battle against cyber threats.

Chapter 10: Securing Wireless Networks Against Advanced Threats

In the ever-evolving landscape of cybersecurity, proactivity is the key to safeguarding systems, data, and sensitive information. Rather than waiting for cyber threats to materialize and cause damage, organizations and individuals can adopt proactive security measures and risk mitigation strategies to stay one step ahead of potential attackers.

One of the fundamental principles of proactive security is the continuous assessment of vulnerabilities within an organization's infrastructure. Vulnerability management involves identifying weaknesses in systems, applications, and configurations that could be exploited by malicious actors. Regular vulnerability scanning and assessment help organizations prioritize and remediate potential risks before they can be leveraged in an attack.

Security awareness training is another essential component of proactive security. Educating employees and users about cybersecurity best practices, threats, and social engineering tactics empowers them to recognize and respond to potential risks. An informed workforce can act as a human firewall, reducing the likelihood of falling victim to phishing, malware, or other cyberattacks.

Implementing robust access controls and authentication mechanisms is crucial for protecting sensitive data and systems. Proactive security measures include enforcing the principle of least privilege, ensuring that users have only the access and permissions necessary for their roles. Multi-factor authentication (MFA) adds an additional layer of security by requiring users to provide multiple forms of verification before accessing accounts or systems.

Security patch management is a critical proactive measure to keep software and systems up to date. Cyber attackers often target known vulnerabilities for which patches have been released. Regularly applying patches and updates helps close these security gaps and reduce the attack surface. Automated patch management solutions can streamline this process, ensuring that systems remain protected against known threats.

The proactive monitoring of network traffic and system logs is essential for detecting and responding to suspicious activities. Security information and event management (SIEM) systems can aggregate and correlate log data from various sources, enabling security teams to identify anomalies and potential security incidents. Real-time alerts and automated responses further enhance the ability to respond swiftly to threats.

Intrusion detection systems (IDS) and intrusion prevention systems (IPS) are proactive security tools that can identify and block malicious activity in real time. These systems use signature-based detection, behavioral analysis, and anomaly detection to spot and mitigate potential threats. When configured properly, IDS and IPS can prevent attacks from progressing beyond the initial stages.

Advanced threat intelligence feeds provide valuable information about emerging threats, vulnerabilities, and attack techniques. Proactively subscribing to threat intelligence services allows organizations to stay informed about the latest threats and adjust their security measures accordingly. Threat intelligence sharing within the cybersecurity community can also provide early warnings and insights into evolving risks.

Security audits and penetration testing are proactive exercises that organizations can undertake to assess their security posture. Conducting regular audits and engaging in ethical hacking exercises help identify weaknesses and gaps in security controls. By simulating real-world attack scenarios, organizations can proactively address vulnerabilities before they can be exploited by malicious actors.

Data encryption and data loss prevention (DLP) solutions are proactive measures for safeguarding sensitive information. Encrypting data at rest and in transit helps protect it from unauthorized access, even in the event of a breach. DLP solutions can monitor and prevent the unauthorized transfer of sensitive data, adding an additional layer of protection.

Zero-trust security frameworks take a proactive approach by assuming that no entity, whether internal or external, should be trusted by default. Instead, zero-trust models require continuous verification of identities and devices before granting access to resources. This approach minimizes the risk of lateral movement by attackers within a network.

Incident response planning and tabletop exercises are proactive measures that organizations can take to prepare for security incidents. By developing detailed response plans and conducting simulated incident scenarios, organizations can ensure that their teams know how to react effectively in the event of a breach. Proactive incident response can help mitigate the impact and recovery time.

The proactive sharing of cybersecurity information and best practices within industries and communities can strengthen collective defenses against cyber threats. Collaborative efforts, such as information sharing and analysis centers (ISACs), enable organizations to pool their knowledge and resources to proactively address common threats and vulnerabilities.

In summary, proactive security measures and risk mitigation strategies are essential for staying ahead of the ever-evolving landscape of cyber threats. By continuously assessing vulnerabilities, educating users, enforcing access controls, applying patches, monitoring network traffic, and engaging in proactive security practices, organizations and individuals can bolster their defenses and reduce the likelihood of falling victim to cyberattacks.

In the realm of cybersecurity, preparation is not solely about addressing today's threats but also about anticipating and readying defenses for emerging threats and future challenges. The cybersecurity landscape is dynamic and ever-evolving, requiring a forward-thinking approach to stay ahead of potential risks.

To prepare for emerging threats, organizations must first establish a robust foundation of security practices. This includes implementing strong access controls, network segmentation, and data encryption to protect sensitive assets. These fundamental measures serve as the building blocks for more advanced security strategies.

One crucial aspect of preparation is staying informed about emerging threats and vulnerabilities. Cyber threat intelligence feeds and information sharing forums provide valuable insights into the latest attack techniques and vulnerabilities. By monitoring these sources, organizations can proactively adjust their security measures to counter new threats.

Machine learning and artificial intelligence (AI) play an increasingly significant role in cybersecurity. These technologies can analyze vast amounts of data to identify patterns and anomalies that may indicate cyber threats. Organizations should consider adopting AI-driven security solutions to enhance their ability to detect and respond to emerging threats.

Security awareness training is an ongoing effort to educate employees and users about the latest threats and best practices. It's vital to keep personnel informed about the evolving tactics used by cybercriminals, such as phishing, social engineering, and ransomware. Regular training empowers individuals to recognize and report potential threats, reducing the organization's overall risk.

Red teaming and penetration testing are proactive measures organizations can take to simulate real-world attacks and assess their security posture. Engaging ethical hackers to identify vulnerabilities and weaknesses allows organizations to rectify issues before malicious actors can exploit them.

The internet of things (IoT) and the proliferation of connected devices present a new frontier for cybersecurity. Organizations must prepare for the security challenges posed by the increasing number of IoT devices. This includes securing devices, monitoring their traffic, and ensuring they don't become entry points for attackers.

Cloud computing continues to gain prominence, and organizations should prepare for the unique security challenges it presents. Cloud security involves not only choosing reputable cloud providers but also configuring and managing cloud resources securely. Encryption, access controls, and monitoring are key elements of cloud security.

Zero-day vulnerabilities—previously unknown software flaws—are particularly challenging to defend against. Organizations should establish rapid response processes for identifying and patching zero-day vulnerabilities as soon as they are discovered. Collaborating with software vendors and security researchers can help expedite the patching process.

Supply chain attacks have become more prevalent, making it crucial for organizations to prepare for this type of threat. Ensuring the security of the entire supply chain, from hardware manufacturers to software developers, is essential. Organizations should assess the security practices of their suppliers and demand transparency in their processes.

The growing complexity of hybrid and multi-cloud environments requires organizations to adapt their security strategies. This includes implementing consistent security policies across on-premises and cloud environments and leveraging cloud-native security tools.

Quantum computing, though still in its infancy, has the potential to disrupt existing encryption methods. Organizations should prepare for the eventual arrival of quantum computers by researching and adopting quantum-resistant encryption algorithms.

The rise of nation-state-sponsored cyberattacks poses a unique challenge. Organizations may become collateral damage in international conflicts, making it essential to develop contingency plans and collaborate with government agencies for threat intelligence sharing.

As technology advances, so do the capabilities of cybercriminals. Organizations must prepare for increasingly sophisticated attack techniques, such as AI-driven attacks, deepfake threats, and advanced evasion tactics.

Preparation for emerging threats should be an ongoing and adaptive process. Cybersecurity teams must continuously assess their security posture, adapt to new technologies and threats, and refine their incident response plans. Collaboration with industry peers and information sharing communities can provide valuable insights and support in this endeavor.

In summary, preparing for emerging threats and future challenges in cybersecurity requires a proactive and adaptable approach. By staying informed, leveraging advanced technologies, enhancing security practices, and collaborating with others, organizations can strengthen their defenses against the evolving threat landscape.

BOOK 4
WIRELESS NETWORK MASTERY
EXPERT-LEVEL PENETRATION TESTING AND DEFENSE

ROB BOTWRIGHT

Chapter 1: Expert Wireless Network Security Landscape

In the ever-evolving landscape of wireless security, staying ahead of emerging threats is of paramount importance. As technology continues to advance, so do the tactics and techniques employed by malicious actors, making it essential for experts in wireless security to be vigilant and adaptable.

One emerging threat in the realm of wireless security is the increasing sophistication of attacks on Wi-Fi networks. Attackers are continuously developing new methods to infiltrate wireless networks, often leveraging advanced tools and techniques. This necessitates a comprehensive understanding of these evolving attack vectors to defend against them effectively.

One such emerging threat is the use of artificial intelligence (AI) and machine learning (ML) by cybercriminals. AI-driven attacks can adapt in real-time, making them particularly challenging to detect and mitigate. Wireless security experts must develop countermeasures that can identify and respond to AI-powered attacks swiftly.

The proliferation of IoT (Internet of Things) devices presents another significant challenge. These devices often have limited security features and can serve as entry points for attackers. Experts must consider the security implications of IoT in network design and implement measures to secure these devices effectively.

5G technology, with its increased speed and connectivity, offers numerous benefits but also introduces new security concerns. The expanded attack surface and potential vulnerabilities in 5G networks demand a thorough understanding of this technology to protect against emerging threats.

Eavesdropping attacks, such as the recently discovered Kr00k vulnerability, highlight the ongoing need to secure wireless communications. Wireless security experts must continually assess and address vulnerabilities in encryption protocols to prevent data interception.

With the rise of remote work, mobile device security has become a critical concern. Attackers target smartphones and tablets to gain unauthorized access to corporate networks or steal sensitive data. Protecting mobile devices through robust security policies and measures is essential.

Phishing attacks, a long-standing threat, continue to evolve. Wireless security experts must educate users about the latest phishing tactics and implement email filtering and monitoring systems to detect and block phishing attempts.

Social engineering attacks remain a potent threat in wireless security. Attackers use psychological manipulation to trick individuals into revealing sensitive information or performing actions that compromise security. Expert wireless security measures should include comprehensive training to recognize and resist social engineering tactics.

As wireless networks become more complex and interconnected, supply chain attacks have gained prominence. Malicious actors target vulnerabilities in the supply chain to compromise hardware or software components. Wireless security experts should work closely with vendors and suppliers to mitigate these risks.

Zero-day vulnerabilities, which are previously unknown software flaws, pose a constant threat. Wireless security experts must have processes in place to identify and respond to zero-day vulnerabilities swiftly, collaborating with vendors for timely patches.

The adoption of cloud services has introduced new attack surfaces and risks. Wireless security experts must ensure that cloud environments are configured securely, with strong access controls and encryption to protect sensitive data.

Credential stuffing attacks, where attackers use stolen usernames and passwords from one breach to gain unauthorized access to other accounts, are on the rise. Implementing multi-factor authentication (MFA) and monitoring for unusual login activity are crucial countermeasures.

Ransomware attacks continue to plague organizations, with attackers increasingly targeting critical infrastructure and demanding higher ransoms. Wireless security experts should focus on robust backup and recovery strategies to minimize the impact of ransomware incidents.

Nation-state-sponsored cyberattacks represent a significant and persistent threat. These attacks often have political motivations and can target a wide range of industries and organizations. Collaborating with government agencies for threat intelligence sharing and response planning is essential.

Deepfake technology, which can create highly convincing fake audio and video, poses a novel threat to wireless security. Experts must be vigilant for potential deepfake attacks that could undermine trust and deceive individuals.

Quantum computing, while still in its early stages, has the potential to break current encryption methods. Wireless security experts must explore and implement quantum-resistant encryption algorithms to protect against future quantum threats.

In summary, emerging threats in expert wireless security require a proactive and adaptable approach. Security professionals must stay informed about the latest attack techniques, leverage advanced technologies, and continually assess and enhance security measures to defend against evolving threats. By remaining vigilant and collaborating with peers and industry experts, wireless security experts can help safeguard wireless networks and data in an increasingly connected world.

Artificial intelligence (AI) and machine learning (ML) have become prominent players in the field of security in recent years. These cutting-edge technologies offer a new dimension to how we approach safeguarding systems and data, enabling security professionals to detect and respond to threats more effectively.

One of the key advantages of AI and ML in security is their ability to process vast amounts of data at speeds that would be impossible for humans to achieve. This capability is especially critical in today's digital landscape, where the volume of data generated by organizations continues to grow exponentially.

AI and ML algorithms excel at identifying patterns and anomalies within data. In the context of security, this means they can analyze network traffic, user behavior, and system logs to detect unusual activities that may indicate a security breach.

Machine learning models can be trained to recognize both known and unknown threats. Traditional security systems often rely on known signatures or patterns of known attacks, leaving them vulnerable to novel, zero-day threats. AI and ML can adapt and learn from new data, making them more capable of identifying previously unseen attacks.

Behavior-based anomaly detection is an area where AI and ML shine. By learning the typical behavior of users and systems, these technologies can flag any deviations from the norm. For example, if a user suddenly starts accessing sensitive files they've never accessed before, AI and ML can recognize this as suspicious activity.

Another significant application of AI and ML in security is in the realm of malware detection. These technologies can analyze files and code to identify potentially malicious elements, even if the malware has never been encountered before. This proactive approach can help organizations defend against emerging threats.

Intrusion detection and prevention systems (IDPS) benefit greatly from AI and ML. These systems can monitor network traffic in real-time and detect signs of intrusions or suspicious behavior. With machine learning, IDPS can become more accurate over time, reducing false positives and improving security incident response.

AI and ML can enhance user authentication methods. Biometric authentication, such as facial recognition or fingerprint scanning, is made more secure with machine learning algorithms that can distinguish between genuine biometric data and spoofed attempts.

Security information and event management (SIEM) systems, which collect and analyze security data from various sources, can leverage AI and ML to improve threat detection and incident response. These technologies can prioritize alerts based on their severity and likelihood of being genuine threats.

AI-driven security analytics can help security teams make sense of the massive amounts of data generated by various security tools. This, in turn, allows for faster and more informed decision-making during security incidents.

The use of AI and ML in security extends to vulnerability management. These technologies can help identify and prioritize vulnerabilities in an organization's systems and applications, ensuring that the most critical issues are addressed promptly.

AI and ML are instrumental in fraud detection and prevention. In the financial sector, for instance, these technologies can analyze transaction data to identify unusual patterns that may indicate fraudulent activity.

Security orchestration, automation, and response (SOAR) platforms benefit from AI and ML by streamlining incident response processes. These platforms can automate repetitive tasks and provide security analysts with actionable insights to resolve incidents more efficiently.

AI and ML also play a significant role in threat intelligence. They can analyze vast amounts of data from various sources, including the dark web, to identify emerging threats and provide organizations with timely information to bolster their defenses.

Despite their many advantages, it's important to note that AI and ML are not without challenges in the security realm. They can generate false positives, and their effectiveness depends on the quality of the data they are trained on. Moreover, they may become targets themselves, as attackers seek to manipulate AI and ML systems to evade detection.

In summary, AI and ML are revolutionizing the field of security by offering advanced capabilities in threat detection, incident response, and vulnerability management. These technologies enable organizations to stay one step ahead of cyber threats in an increasingly complex and dynamic digital landscape. While challenges exist, the benefits of incorporating AI and ML into security strategies are undeniable, making them indispensable tools for safeguarding critical assets and data.

Chapter 2: Cutting-Edge Wi-Fi Protocols and Security Features

As we delve into the future of Wi-Fi security, it's essential to recognize that the landscape of wireless networking is continually evolving to keep up with emerging threats and vulnerabilities. While WPA3 has made significant strides in enhancing the security of Wi-Fi networks, it's not the end of the road. In this chapter, we will explore the protocols and technologies that are expected to shape the future of Wi-Fi security.

One of the primary driving forces behind the development of new security protocols is the ever-increasing sophistication of cyber threats. Attackers are becoming more adept at exploiting vulnerabilities and bypassing existing security measures. Consequently, the Wi-Fi industry must adapt and innovate to stay ahead of malicious actors.

One of the emerging technologies that hold promise for the future of Wi-Fi security is Wi-Fi 6E. This latest iteration of Wi-Fi technology not only offers faster speeds and reduced latency but also introduces enhancements in security. Wi-Fi 6E operates in the 6 GHz band, providing more spectrum for less interference. This additional spectrum can be leveraged for security purposes, allowing for better isolation of Wi-Fi networks and reducing the risk of interference from neighboring networks.

In addition to Wi-Fi 6E, the Wi-Fi Alliance is actively working on the development of WPA3 enhancements. These enhancements are designed to address known vulnerabilities and provide even stronger protection for Wi-Fi networks. The Wi-Fi Alliance's commitment to ongoing security improvements is a positive sign for the future of Wi-Fi security. The concept of "zero-trust" security is gaining traction in the Wi-Fi industry. Zero-trust security operates on the principle of "never trust, always verify." In the context of Wi-Fi, this means that devices and users are never assumed to be trustworthy, and continuous verification of their identity and security posture is required. Implementing zero-trust security in Wi-Fi networks involves rigorous access controls, multi-factor authentication, and constant monitoring of network activity. Another notable development in Wi-Fi security is the increasing adoption of machine learning and artificial intelligence. These technologies are being used to analyze network traffic in real-time and identify patterns indicative of cyber threats. By leveraging AI and ML, Wi-Fi security systems can automatically respond to emerging threats, mitigating risks more effectively. The use of hardware-based security features in Wi-Fi devices is also on the rise. Chip manufacturers are embedding security mechanisms directly into Wi-Fi hardware, making it more challenging for attackers to compromise devices at a low level. These hardware-based security measures include secure boot processes and hardware-based encryption.

Quantum computing is on the horizon, and it poses a potential threat to existing encryption algorithms. As quantum computers become more powerful, they could potentially break the encryption used in current Wi-Fi security protocols. To address this concern, researchers are working on developing quantum-resistant encryption algorithms that can withstand attacks from quantum computers. The adoption of these quantum-resistant algorithms will be a crucial aspect of future Wi-Fi security.

The proliferation of the Internet of Things (IoT) devices presents unique security challenges for Wi-Fi networks. Many IoT devices have limited processing power and memory, making it difficult to implement robust security measures. Future Wi-Fi security protocols will need to address the specific requirements of IoT devices to ensure their protection. The evolution of Wi-Fi security is not solely dependent on technological advancements but also on industry standards and regulatory frameworks. Governments and regulatory bodies are increasingly recognizing the importance of cybersecurity and are implementing regulations to ensure the security of wireless networks. Compliance with these regulations will be a driving force behind the adoption of advanced security protocols. In summary, the future of Wi-Fi security is marked by a commitment to staying ahead of evolving threats. Technologies such as Wi-Fi 6E, enhanced WPA3, zero-trust security, machine learning, hardware-based security, quantum-resistant encryption, and IoT-specific security measures are all contributing to a more robust and resilient Wi-Fi security landscape. As we embrace these innovations, we can look forward to a future where Wi-Fi networks are more secure and better equipped to protect against emerging cyber threats. In the ever-evolving landscape of wireless security, implementing advanced security features is a crucial step in fortifying your Wi-Fi network against an array of threats. These features go beyond the basics, providing additional layers of protection that can thwart even the most determined adversaries. As we explore these advanced security measures, you'll gain insights into how to safeguard your network effectively.

One of the fundamental pillars of advanced security is the utilization of robust encryption protocols. While WPA3 has significantly improved encryption in Wi-Fi networks, there are additional measures you can take to enhance this aspect of security. Implementing end-to-end encryption, particularly for sensitive data transmissions, ensures that even if an attacker gains access to your network, they won't be able to decipher the encrypted data.

Segmentation is another advanced security feature that plays a vital role in minimizing the attack surface of your network. By dividing your network into separate segments or VLANs (Virtual Local Area Networks), you can restrict access to specific resources and limit lateral movement in case of a breach. This approach is particularly effective in environments where different user groups or devices require different levels of access.

Advanced firewalls and intrusion detection/prevention systems are indispensable tools for protecting your Wi-Fi network. Next-generation firewalls (NGFWs) go beyond traditional firewalls by inspecting traffic at the application layer, allowing for more granular control and threat detection. Intrusion detection and prevention systems (IDPS) monitor network traffic for suspicious activity and can automatically block or mitigate threats in real-time.

Regular security assessments and penetration testing are key components of advanced security. Conducting these assessments periodically allows you to proactively identify vulnerabilities and weaknesses in your network's security posture. Ethical hackers or security professionals can simulate attacks, helping you uncover potential risks before malicious actors exploit them.

Multi-factor authentication (MFA) is a simple yet powerful security feature that adds an extra layer of protection to user accounts. By requiring users to provide two or more forms of authentication, such as a password and a one-time code sent to their mobile device, you significantly reduce the risk of unauthorized access, even if credentials are compromised. Network Access Control (NAC) is an advanced security mechanism that ensures only authorized devices gain access to your Wi-Fi network. NAC solutions can assess the security posture of connecting devices, checking for up-to-date antivirus software, patches, and compliance with security policies before granting access. Any device that fails to meet the criteria is quarantined or denied network access.

Advanced threat intelligence feeds are invaluable for staying informed about the latest cyber threats and vulnerabilities. Subscribing to threat intelligence services or utilizing open-source threat feeds can help your organization proactively defend against emerging threats. These feeds provide real-time information on malicious IP addresses, domains, and attack techniques.

Implementing a Security Information and Event Management (SIEM) system can help your organization centralize the collection, analysis, and correlation of security event data from various sources. SIEM platforms provide real-time insights into network activity, helping security teams detect and respond to threats more effectively. They can also generate alerts and reports to facilitate incident investigation.

Regularly updating and patching all network devices and software is a basic but often overlooked aspect of advanced security. Vulnerabilities can arise from outdated firmware, operating systems, or applications, making your network an easy target for attackers. Automated patch management systems can streamline this process, ensuring that security updates are promptly applied.

Behavioral analytics is an advanced security feature that leverages machine learning to detect anomalies in user and device behavior. By establishing a baseline of normal behavior, the system can identify deviations that may indicate a security threat. For example, if a user suddenly accesses resources they've never used before, it could be a sign of a compromised account.

Implementing a robust incident response plan is essential for mitigating the impact of security incidents. Advanced security features alone cannot guarantee absolute protection, so having a well-defined plan that outlines how to respond to security breaches, recover from them, and communicate with stakeholders is critical.

Finally, security awareness and training for your organization's staff are vital components of advanced security. Human error remains a significant factor in security breaches, so educating employees about best practices, social engineering tactics, and the importance of vigilance can significantly reduce the risk of successful attacks.

Incorporating these advanced security features into your Wi-Fi network strategy can help you create a resilient and highly secure environment. While no system is entirely impervious to threats, these measures collectively strengthen your defenses and provide a robust foundation for safeguarding your wireless network.

Chapter 3: Advanced Wireless Reconnaissance and Target Profiling

Passive reconnaissance and advanced OSINT (Open-Source Intelligence) techniques are essential components of modern cybersecurity, providing invaluable insights into potential targets and vulnerabilities. In this chapter, we'll delve into the intricacies of passive reconnaissance and explore how OSINT can be leveraged for a deeper understanding of your adversaries and their tactics.

Passive reconnaissance, also known as footprinting, is the initial phase of an ethical hacking or cybersecurity assessment. It involves gathering information about a target without directly interacting with it. This approach is non-intrusive and aims to minimize the risk of detection. Passive reconnaissance primarily relies on publicly available information, making it a valuable technique for both ethical hackers and cybercriminals.

One of the primary sources of information for passive reconnaissance is the domain name system (DNS). By querying DNS servers, an attacker can discover various domains associated with a target organization. Subdomains, mail servers, and external services can all be identified through DNS queries, providing a foundation for further exploration.

Search engines are another critical resource for passive reconnaissance. Utilizing advanced search operators, attackers can unearth a wealth of information about a target, including web pages, documents, and even configuration files. Google Dorks, for example, are specific search queries that can reveal sensitive information inadvertently exposed by a target.

Social media platforms are rich repositories of information for passive reconnaissance. Individuals often share details about their organizations, job roles, and even network configurations on platforms like LinkedIn, Twitter, and Facebook. Ethical hackers can use this information to create accurate target profiles.

Publicly available documents and files, such as PDFs, Word documents, and spreadsheets, can contain hidden gems of information. Metadata within these files may reveal author names, revision history, and sometimes even sensitive data that wasn't intended for public consumption.

Passive DNS analysis can uncover historical DNS records associated with a target, revealing changes in infrastructure and potentially identifying deprecated services or subdomains. By analyzing these records, ethical hackers can gain insights into a target's digital evolution.

WHOIS databases provide information about domain registrations, including the names and contact details of registrants. This data can be useful for determining the ownership of a domain or identifying potential threat actors.

Reverse IP lookup tools enable ethical hackers to discover other websites hosted on the same server as the target. This information can reveal shared hosting environments and potential attack vectors.

While passive reconnaissance primarily focuses on information gathering, advanced OSINT techniques take it a step further by applying analytical and investigative skills. OSINT encompasses a wide range of sources, from publicly available databases to specialized search engines and forums.

Specialized OSINT tools and platforms like Shodan and Censys allow ethical hackers to search for specific devices and services connected to the internet. These tools can uncover open ports, vulnerable services, and even exposed industrial control systems.

Publicly accessible databases, such as the Common Vulnerabilities and Exposures (CVE) database, provide information about known vulnerabilities. Ethical hackers can use OSINT to cross-reference target systems with these databases, identifying potential weaknesses.

Deep web and dark web exploration are advanced OSINT techniques that can reveal hidden information not indexed by traditional search engines. These areas of the internet may contain forums, marketplaces, and communication channels where cybercriminals discuss tactics, share tools, and plan attacks.

Advanced OSINT practitioners may employ custom scripts and automation to scrape and analyze vast amounts of data from various sources. This process, known as data aggregation, can help uncover hidden patterns and relationships among different data points.

Link analysis, a technique used in advanced OSINT, involves mapping connections between individuals, organizations, and online entities. By visualizing these connections, ethical hackers can identify potential threat actors and their relationships.

Passive reconnaissance and advanced OSINT techniques are foundational to ethical hacking and cybersecurity.

They empower security professionals to understand their adversaries, identify potential vulnerabilities, and proactively defend against cyber threats. By continuously honing these skills, ethical hackers can stay one step ahead of cybercriminals and protect the digital landscape.

In the realm of cybersecurity and ethical hacking, advanced target profiling strategies serve as a critical foundation for understanding potential adversaries and their vulnerabilities. This chapter delves into the intricacies of these strategies, exploring how they enable security professionals to develop comprehensive profiles of their targets.

Advanced target profiling goes beyond surface-level information gathering. It involves a systematic and in-depth analysis of every aspect related to a target, whether it's an organization, individual, or system. The primary objective is to acquire a nuanced understanding of the target's digital footprint, weaknesses, and potential attack vectors.

One fundamental aspect of advanced target profiling is the identification of key stakeholders within an organization. Ethical hackers aim to discover the roles and responsibilities of individuals or teams, as this information can help in crafting more targeted and effective attacks.

Analyzing an organization's online presence is crucial for understanding its operations and potential vulnerabilities. This includes scrutinizing its websites, social media accounts, forums, and any other digital assets. Even seemingly innocuous information like employee job listings or event announcements can reveal valuable insights.

Network infrastructure mapping plays a pivotal role in advanced target profiling. Ethical hackers aim to identify all network devices, services, and connections, whether they are visible on the public internet or hidden within private networks. This knowledge assists in pinpointing potential attack vectors.

Furthermore, understanding an organization's digital supply chain is essential. This involves tracing the relationships and dependencies with external vendors, partners, and service providers. A compromise in any of these interconnected entities can impact the target organization's security.

Advanced target profiling extends to identifying technology stacks and software used by the target. This knowledge can help ethical hackers pinpoint known vulnerabilities associated with specific technologies, such as outdated software or unpatched systems.

Analyzing a target's online communication and information-sharing practices is vital. Ethical hackers explore how an organization exchanges data and how employees collaborate. This information can uncover potential weak points where sensitive data might be exposed or intercepted.

Advanced profiling also delves into the target's security posture. Ethical hackers assess the effectiveness of existing security measures, including firewalls, intrusion detection systems, and access controls. Understanding these defenses aids in devising strategies to bypass or exploit them.

The gathering of historical data is an integral part of advanced profiling. Security professionals aim to uncover past security incidents, breaches, or vulnerabilities that may have affected the target. This historical context provides insights into recurring issues and areas that may require heightened scrutiny.

Social engineering vectors are another critical aspect of advanced target profiling. Ethical hackers aim to understand the human element of security, identifying potential entry points via tactics like phishing, pretexting, or baiting.

The geographical and geopolitical context of a target also factors into advanced profiling. Understanding the location and jurisdiction in which the target operates can impact the choice of attack vectors and the potential repercussions of cyber activities.

Furthermore, ethical hackers must consider legal and compliance aspects in their profiling efforts. Compliance requirements, industry regulations, and data protection laws may influence the target's security measures and vulnerabilities.

Advanced target profiling is a dynamic process that evolves alongside the target and the threat landscape. It involves continuous monitoring and adaptation to uncover new vulnerabilities, changes in the target's infrastructure, or emerging threats.

To execute advanced profiling effectively, ethical hackers often leverage a wide range of tools and resources. These may include specialized software for network scanning, reconnaissance, and vulnerability assessment, as well as OSINT tools and frameworks.

Ethical hackers must always exercise caution and adhere to ethical guidelines while conducting advanced target profiling. Unauthorized access or data breaches can have severe legal and ethical consequences.

In summary, advanced target profiling strategies are essential for ethical hackers and security professionals in their mission to safeguard digital assets and protect against cyber threats. By employing a systematic and comprehensive approach, they can develop a detailed understanding of their targets, identify potential vulnerabilities, and proactively defend against emerging risks.

Chapter 4: Zero-Day Exploitation of Wireless Vulnerabilities

In the realm of cybersecurity and ethical hacking, one of the most challenging yet critical tasks is discovering and exploiting unknown vulnerabilities in systems, applications, and networks. These vulnerabilities, often referred to as "zero-day" vulnerabilities, are flaws or weaknesses that are unknown to the vendor or developer, leaving them unpatched and open to exploitation. Ethical hackers play a crucial role in identifying and mitigating these vulnerabilities to enhance overall security.

The process of discovering unknown vulnerabilities begins with a deep understanding of software, hardware, and network protocols. Ethical hackers often have to think like attackers, trying to uncover weaknesses that may not be apparent to the average user or even the system's administrators.

One common approach to discovering unknown vulnerabilities is through fuzz testing or fuzzing. Fuzzing involves sending random or unexpected input data to a software application to observe how it behaves. By doing this, ethical hackers can sometimes trigger crashes or abnormal behavior that indicates the presence of a vulnerability.

Another technique employed in vulnerability discovery is reverse engineering. This involves dissecting software or firmware to understand its inner workings, with the goal of identifying potential weaknesses or vulnerabilities. Reverse engineering can be a painstaking process but can yield valuable insights into a system's security.

Ethical hackers also keep a close eye on public and private sources of information, such as underground forums, dark web marketplaces, and vulnerability databases. Information about zero-day vulnerabilities is sometimes traded or sold in these spaces, and by monitoring them, ethical hackers can gain early access to information about potential threats.

Collaboration and knowledge sharing within the cybersecurity community are essential for discovering unknown vulnerabilities. Ethical hackers often participate in bug bounty programs, where organizations offer rewards for identifying and responsibly disclosing security flaws. These programs incentivize ethical hackers to actively search for vulnerabilities and report them to the affected organizations.

Sometimes, zero-day vulnerabilities are discovered inadvertently while conducting security assessments or penetration testing. During these assessments, ethical hackers simulate real-world attacks on systems and applications, and in the process, they may stumble upon previously unknown weaknesses.

Once an unknown vulnerability is identified, ethical hackers face a critical ethical dilemma. They must decide whether to responsibly disclose the vulnerability to the affected organization or exploit it for malicious purposes. The ethical choice is always to report the vulnerability promptly so that the organization can take measures to patch or mitigate it.

Responsible disclosure is a fundamental principle in the world of ethical hacking. When a vulnerability is discovered, ethical hackers typically follow a structured process to report it to the organization responsible for the software or system. This process often involves providing a detailed description of the vulnerability, proof of concept, and recommendations for mitigation.

In some cases, organizations may not respond promptly or effectively to vulnerability reports. This can be challenging for ethical hackers who are committed to improving security. However, the responsible disclosure process encourages patience and persistence in working with organizations to address vulnerabilities.

Once a vulnerability is disclosed and the organization is working on a patch, ethical hackers may assist in the mitigation process. They can offer insights and guidance on how to secure the affected system, reducing the risk of exploitation while the patch is being developed and deployed.

Ethical hackers should always prioritize the greater good and adhere to ethical standards when dealing with unknown vulnerabilities. Exploiting these vulnerabilities for personal gain or malicious purposes is not only unethical but also illegal.

The responsible disclosure of unknown vulnerabilities ultimately contributes to the overall improvement of cybersecurity. As vulnerabilities are identified and patched, systems become more resilient to attacks, and organizations can better protect their data and infrastructure.

In summary, discovering and exploiting unknown vulnerabilities is a complex and challenging aspect of ethical hacking. Ethical hackers use a combination of techniques, including fuzz testing, reverse engineering, monitoring online sources, and participating in bug bounty programs, to uncover these vulnerabilities. The responsible disclosure of these vulnerabilities is essential to enhance cybersecurity and protect organizations from potential threats. Ethical hackers play a crucial role in making the digital world safer for everyone.

Coordinated Vulnerability Disclosure (CVD) is a structured and responsible approach to handling security vulnerabilities in software, hardware, or systems. It is a vital aspect of the cybersecurity landscape, aiming to minimize the risks associated with vulnerabilities by facilitating communication and collaboration between the security community and the organizations or vendors responsible for the affected products or services.

The primary goal of CVD is to ensure that security vulnerabilities are addressed promptly and efficiently, reducing the potential harm they can cause. To understand CVD fully, it's essential to explore its key components and the various stakeholders involved in the process.

At the heart of CVD is the concept of responsible disclosure. This means that when a security researcher or ethical hacker discovers a vulnerability, they responsibly disclose it to the affected organization or vendor. Responsible disclosure entails providing detailed information about the vulnerability, including its nature, potential impact, and proof of concept.

When a vulnerability is reported, the affected organization plays a crucial role in the CVD process. They are responsible for acknowledging the report, assessing the severity of the vulnerability, and developing a plan to mitigate or patch it. Effective communication between the reporting party and the organization is essential to ensure that the vulnerability is properly understood and addressed.

In some cases, vulnerabilities may be assigned a Common Vulnerability Scoring System (CVSS) score, which quantifies the potential impact and exploitability of the vulnerability. This score helps organizations prioritize their response efforts, focusing on the most critical vulnerabilities first.

Coordinated Vulnerability Disclosure also involves the establishment of a timeline for addressing the vulnerability. While security researchers are generally encouraged to report vulnerabilities as soon as possible, organizations need time to investigate, develop patches, and test them thoroughly. Transparency and open communication regarding the timeline are essential to manage expectations.

Once a patch or mitigation strategy is ready, the organization releases it to the public. This information allows users and administrators to protect their systems by applying the necessary updates or implementing recommended mitigations. Organizations are encouraged to provide clear and concise guidance on how to remediate the vulnerability.

It's important to note that not all vulnerabilities are immediately patched. In some cases, organizations may need more time to develop a comprehensive solution. In such situations, they may recommend temporary workarounds or mitigations to reduce the risk until a full patch is available.

The security researcher or ethical hacker who discovered the vulnerability also plays a critical role in the CVD process. They are encouraged to work collaboratively with the affected organization, assisting with any additional information or clarification needed to understand the vulnerability fully. This cooperation ensures that the organization can address the issue effectively.

In cases where an organization is unresponsive or unable to address the vulnerability, the researcher may choose to involve a Computer Emergency Response Team (CERT) or a similar coordinating entity. These organizations specialize in managing and coordinating the disclosure of security vulnerabilities.

The ultimate goal of Coordinated Vulnerability Disclosure is to protect end-users and organizations from potential harm. By working together, the security community and organizations can minimize the window of opportunity for attackers to exploit vulnerabilities. This collaborative approach enhances overall cybersecurity.

Beyond responsible disclosure, there are also coordinated efforts to share information about vulnerabilities with a broader community. Vulnerability databases, such as the Common Vulnerabilities and Exposures (CVE) system, provide a standardized way to catalog and share information about vulnerabilities. This allows organizations and security professionals to track and reference vulnerabilities easily.

CVD is not limited to software or technology vendors. It also applies to hardware manufacturers, service providers, and organizations responsible for critical infrastructure. In an increasingly interconnected world, vulnerabilities in one system can have far-reaching consequences, making CVD a critical practice to protect digital ecosystems.

In summary, Coordinated Vulnerability Disclosure is an essential and responsible approach to managing security vulnerabilities in software, hardware, and systems. It involves the responsible reporting of vulnerabilities, collaboration between security researchers and organizations, and transparent communication with the public. CVD aims to reduce the potential harm caused by vulnerabilities and enhance overall cybersecurity in an interconnected digital landscape.

Chapter 5: Advanced Cryptanalysis and Key Recovery

In the ever-evolving landscape of Wi-Fi networks and their security, advanced cryptographic attacks have emerged as a significant concern for both individuals and organizations. These attacks target the encryption mechanisms that protect data transmitted over Wi-Fi networks, aiming to exploit vulnerabilities and gain unauthorized access. One of the most well-known cryptographic attacks against Wi-Fi networks is the infamous "KRACK" attack, short for Key Reinstallation Attack. In a KRACK attack, an adversary intercepts and manipulates the four-way handshake that occurs when a device attempts to connect to a Wi-Fi network protected by the WPA2 encryption protocol. By exploiting weaknesses in this handshake process, an attacker can force the reuse of encryption keys and subsequently decrypt the traffic between the victim device and the Wi-Fi access point. The KRACK attack raised awareness about the vulnerabilities inherent in widely used Wi-Fi security protocols and prompted improvements in encryption standards. However, cryptographic attacks in Wi-Fi networks extend beyond KRACK, encompassing a range of techniques and vulnerabilities. One such technique is the use of brute-force attacks against encryption keys. A brute-force attack involves systematically trying every possible key until the correct one is found, allowing the attacker to decrypt the data. To mitigate this risk, it's crucial to use strong, complex, and unique encryption keys, making it computationally infeasible for an attacker to guess the correct key within a reasonable time frame. Another cryptographic attack of concern is known as a dictionary attack. In this method, attackers use a precompiled list of commonly used words, phrases, or passwords to guess the encryption key. While similar to a brute-force attack, dictionary attacks are often faster and more efficient, as they target likely key candidates. To counter dictionary attacks, it's essential to use complex, random encryption keys that cannot be easily guessed from common words or patterns. In addition to dictionary attacks, attackers may employ rainbow table attacks. Rainbow tables are precomputed tables of hash values for different possible inputs. Attackers use these tables to reverse engineer hashed encryption keys, potentially revealing the original key. To defend against rainbow table attacks, using techniques like salting, which adds random data to the encryption key before hashing, can make it significantly more challenging for attackers to reverse the process. Advanced cryptographic attacks may also involve leveraging weaknesses in encryption algorithms themselves. For example, if a cryptographic algorithm is found to have mathematical vulnerabilities or flaws, attackers can exploit these weaknesses to decrypt encrypted data. To address this, it's crucial to stay informed about potential vulnerabilities in encryption algorithms and keep Wi-Fi network devices and software up to date with the latest security patches and updates. Cryptographic attacks are not limited to Wi-Fi network traffic interception but also extend to attacks targeting the encryption keys themselves. A side-channel attack is an example of such an attack, where an attacker indirectly obtains encryption keys by analyzing various physical or electrical characteristics of a device during the encryption process. To mitigate side-channel attacks, implementing countermeasures such as hardware-based security modules and secure key storage can add an additional layer of protection. Another advanced cryptographic attack that has garnered attention is the "Bleichenbacher attack" against RSA encryption. This attack targets vulnerabilities in how RSA encryption handles padding in encrypted messages. By exploiting these vulnerabilities, an attacker can gradually recover the RSA private key, allowing them to decrypt encrypted data. To defend against the Bleichenbacher attack and similar vulnerabilities, implementing secure padding schemes and adhering to best practices in RSA encryption is essential. Quantum computing represents another potential avenue for advanced cryptographic attacks against Wi-Fi networks. Quantum computers have the potential to break commonly used encryption algorithms, such as RSA and ECC (Elliptic Curve Cryptography), by leveraging their unique quantum properties. As quantum computing technology advances, the need for post-quantum cryptography, which includes encryption algorithms specifically designed to resist quantum attacks, becomes increasingly critical for securing Wi-Fi networks. The threat landscape for cryptographic attacks in Wi-Fi networks is continually evolving, and attackers are becoming more sophisticated in their techniques. To stay ahead of these threats, it's essential for individuals and organizations to adopt a proactive approach to Wi-Fi security. This includes regularly updating Wi-Fi equipment and software, using strong and unique encryption keys, implementing robust encryption algorithms, and staying informed about emerging cryptographic vulnerabilities and attacks. In summary, advanced cryptographic attacks pose a significant risk to the security of Wi-Fi networks. These attacks encompass a wide range of techniques and vulnerabilities, from brute-force and dictionary attacks to rainbow table attacks and side-channel attacks. Defending against these threats requires a combination of strong encryption practices, secure key management, and awareness of emerging cryptographic vulnerabilities. As technology continues to advance, staying vigilant and proactive in Wi-Fi security is crucial to protect sensitive data and maintain the integrity of wireless networks. Recovering encryption keys and implementing effective key management strategies are crucial aspects of securing sensitive data in Wi-Fi networks. Encryption keys are the foundation of data security in any cryptographic system, including Wi-Fi networks. These keys are used to encrypt and decrypt data, ensuring that it remains confidential and protected from unauthorized access. However, in some situations, there may be a need to recover encryption keys, such as when they are lost, forgotten, or compromised. One common approach to key recovery is through the use of key escrow systems. In a key escrow system, a trusted third party, known as an escrow agent, is responsible for securely storing copies of encryption keys. This allows authorized entities to recover the keys when necessary, such as in cases of data recovery or legal requirements. Key escrow systems are often used in government and enterprise environments where data security and regulatory compliance are paramount. Effective key management is essential for maintaining the security of Wi-Fi networks and preventing unauthorized access to sensitive information. One fundamental aspect of key management is ensuring that encryption keys are generated, stored, and distributed securely. Randomness is a crucial factor in key generation, as predictable keys can be easily guessed or cracked by attackers. Modern cryptographic systems use secure random number generators (RNGs) to create unpredictable keys that are resistant to guessing attacks. These keys should also be of sufficient length to withstand brute-force attacks, where an attacker tries all possible key combinations. Another critical aspect of key management is key storage. Encryption keys must be stored securely to prevent unauthorized access. Hardware security modules (HSMs) are specialized devices designed to store encryption keys in a tamper-resistant and highly secure environment. Using HSMs can protect keys from physical attacks and ensure their confidentiality and integrity. Additionally, organizations should implement access control policies to restrict who can access and use encryption keys. Implementing strong authentication and authorization mechanisms can prevent unauthorized personnel from obtaining or using keys. Key rotation is another key management practice that helps maintain the security of Wi-Fi networks. Regularly changing encryption keys reduces the exposure to potential attacks and limits the impact of a compromised key. Key rotation schedules should be carefully planned to minimize disruption to network operations while maintaining security. In cases where encryption keys need to be recovered, several techniques and strategies can be employed. One common method for key recovery is to use backup copies of encryption keys stored in secure locations. These backup copies are typically stored in a manner that ensures their confidentiality and integrity, such as in a secure vault or an HSM. In the event of key loss or compromise, the backup copies can be used to restore access to encrypted data. Another approach to key recovery is the use of key derivation functions (KDFs). KDFs are cryptographic algorithms designed to generate encryption keys from a master key or passphrase. By using the same master key or passphrase and the same KDF, it is possible to derive the same encryption key, allowing for key recovery. However, it's important to securely manage and protect the master key or passphrase to prevent unauthorized key recovery. Some cryptographic systems also support key splitting, where encryption keys are divided into multiple parts or shares. Each share is distributed to different individuals or entities, and a certain threshold of shares is required to reconstruct the original key. This approach enhances security by reducing the risk of a single point of failure or compromise. When key recovery is necessary, authorized parties can combine their shares to reconstruct the encryption key. The process of recovering encryption keys should be well-documented and follow established procedures to ensure that it is done securely and in compliance with applicable regulations. Key management and key recovery are integral parts of a comprehensive security strategy for Wi-Fi networks. By implementing strong key generation, secure key storage, access control policies, and key rotation practices, organizations can effectively protect their data from unauthorized access and recover encryption keys when needed. Additionally, using key escrow systems, backup copies, KDFs, and key splitting techniques provides flexibility and options for key recovery without compromising security. In summary, recovering encryption keys and implementing robust key management practices are essential components of Wi-Fi network security. Encryption keys are the foundation of data protection, and their secure generation, storage, and distribution are critical. Key management encompasses key storage, rotation, and access control to maintain security. When key recovery is necessary, organizations can use backup copies, key derivation functions, or key splitting techniques while following documented procedures to ensure a secure and compliant process. Strong key management and recovery practices are vital for safeguarding sensitive data in Wi-Fi networks.

Chapter 6: Covert and Persistent Attacks on Wi-Fi Networks

Covert communication channels, often referred to simply as covert channels, are a fascinating and somewhat clandestine aspect of information security and network communication. These channels provide a means for data to be transferred between two parties while evading detection by security mechanisms and protocols. The term "covert" implies that these channels operate discreetly, often hidden within seemingly innocuous communication or data flows. Covert channels are used for various purposes, including espionage, cyberattacks, and bypassing security controls. To understand covert channels better, it's essential to delve into their characteristics and the techniques employed in their creation and detection. One of the fundamental characteristics of covert channels is their ability to hide data within seemingly legitimate communication. In other words, covert channels use existing communication pathways or protocols to convey information surreptitiously. This can be achieved by manipulating the timing, ordering, or encoding of data in such a way that it appears normal to anyone monitoring the communication. One classic example of a covert channel is using variations in the timing between packets to transmit hidden data. By slightly delaying or accelerating the transmission of packets, covert data can be encoded and transmitted without raising suspicion. Covert channels can also take advantage of unused or less-monitored parts of a network protocol. For instance, some network protocols may have reserved fields that are not actively used in typical communication. Covert channels can use these fields to encode and transmit data, as long as the receiving party knows how to interpret them. Another characteristic of covert channels is their reliance on a shared protocol or communication medium between the sender and the receiver. Both parties must understand the encoding and decoding methods used in the covert channel to communicate effectively. The sender and receiver often share a predefined set of rules, known as a covert channel protocol, to ensure that data is transmitted accurately and covertly. Detecting covert channels can be a challenging task, as they are intentionally designed to be subtle and avoid detection by standard security mechanisms. Several methods and techniques are employed to identify the presence of covert channels within a network or system. One common approach to covert channel detection is anomaly detection. Anomalies in network traffic, such as unusual packet timing or unexpected data patterns, can be indicators of covert communication. Network monitoring tools and intrusion detection systems (IDS) can be configured to raise alerts when such anomalies are detected. Another detection method involves analyzing the behavior of network protocols and applications. Covert channels may manipulate protocol behaviors, such as unexpected changes in the order or timing of data transmission. Monitoring and analyzing these protocol deviations can reveal the presence of covert channels. Furthermore, statistical analysis and machine learning techniques can be employed to detect patterns associated with covert channels. These methods can identify hidden data patterns within network traffic that might not be apparent through manual inspection. It's important to note that covert channels can be employed both for legitimate purposes and malicious activities. In some cases, organizations may use covert channels to bypass network restrictions or filters for valid reasons, such as security testing or data recovery. However, malicious actors can exploit covert channels to exfiltrate sensitive information, control compromised systems, or carry out cyberattacks. To prevent and mitigate the risks associated with covert channels, organizations should implement robust network monitoring, intrusion detection, and anomaly detection systems. Furthermore, network administrators and security professionals should stay informed about emerging covert channel techniques and employ proactive measures to counteract them. In summary, covert communication channels are a fascinating aspect of information security and network communication. These channels enable data to be transmitted discreetly within existing communication pathways, often evading detection by security mechanisms. Understanding the characteristics and techniques of covert channels is essential for both identifying their presence and defending against their potential misuse. Detection methods, including anomaly detection, protocol analysis, statistical analysis, and machine learning, can help uncover covert channels within a network or system. Organizations must remain vigilant and proactive in addressing covert channels to protect their data and network security. Establishing and maintaining persistent access is a critical aspect of cybersecurity, often employed by threat actors seeking to maintain long-term control over compromised systems. Persistent access, also known as persistence, refers to the ability of an attacker to maintain unauthorized access to a compromised system or network even after the initial breach has occurred. This concept is fundamental to understanding how cyberattacks can evolve into long-term threats. To gain a clearer understanding of establishing and maintaining persistent access, we'll explore the methods, techniques, and countermeasures associated with this aspect of cybersecurity. One common method used to establish persistence is the deployment of malicious software, often referred to as malware, on a compromised system. Malware can come in various forms, including backdoors, rootkits, Trojans, and remote access tools. These malicious programs are designed to run silently in the background, allowing attackers to access the compromised system at will. Once a malware-infected system is compromised, the attacker can return to it whenever they choose, effectively maintaining persistent access. A well-known example of malware that establishes persistence is a Remote Access Trojan (RAT), which allows remote control of the infected system. Another method employed by threat actors to establish and maintain persistent access is the manipulation of system settings and configurations. Attackers may alter system configurations, registry entries, or startup processes to ensure that their malicious code runs automatically every time the compromised system reboots. This ensures that even if the system is restarted or undergoes maintenance, the attacker's access remains intact. Kernel-level rootkits, for instance, can modify the core components of an operating system to conceal malicious activities and maintain access. Social engineering tactics can also be used to establish and maintain persistence. For instance, attackers may trick individuals with privileged access into providing login credentials or installing malware on their systems. This can allow attackers to maintain access to sensitive data and resources. Another technique employed by attackers is the use of Command and Control (C2) servers. These servers serve as communication hubs that allow attackers to remotely control compromised systems. By periodically connecting to these C2 servers, attackers can issue commands and receive data from compromised systems while evading detection. To counter the establishment of persistent access, organizations must employ robust security measures and practices. Regularly updating and patching systems can help prevent attackers from exploiting known vulnerabilities to establish persistence. Network monitoring and intrusion detection systems can also aid in identifying suspicious activity that may indicate the presence of malware or unauthorized access. Implementing strong access controls, such as two-factor authentication and the principle of least privilege, can limit the opportunities for attackers to establish persistence. Moreover, security teams should conduct regular security assessments and penetration testing to identify and remediate vulnerabilities that could be exploited by threat actors. In addition to traditional cybersecurity measures, organizations should also invest in user education and awareness training to help employees recognize and resist social engineering attempts. Establishing and maintaining persistent access is a multifaceted challenge in the realm of cybersecurity. It involves a variety of methods, techniques, and countermeasures employed by both attackers and defenders. By understanding these concepts and implementing effective security measures, organizations can better protect their systems and data from the threat of persistent access by malicious actors. In summary, persistent access is a critical aspect of cybersecurity, with attackers using various methods to maintain unauthorized access to compromised systems. This includes the use of malware, manipulation of system settings, social engineering, and Command and Control (C2) servers. Organizations can counter these threats by regularly updating and patching systems, implementing strong access controls, and providing user education and awareness training. By addressing these aspects, organizations can enhance their security posture and reduce the risk of persistent access by malicious actors.

Chapter 7: Advanced Post-Exploitation and Persistence Mechanisms

Advanced techniques for post-exploitation are a crucial aspect of cybersecurity, allowing security professionals and ethical hackers to understand, mitigate, and respond effectively to cyber threats once an attacker has gained unauthorized access to a system or network. Post-exploitation refers to the actions an attacker takes after successfully compromising a system. These actions can range from maintaining access and privilege escalation to data exfiltration and covering their tracks. In this chapter, we'll delve into advanced post-exploitation techniques, examining both offensive and defensive strategies. One of the primary goals of post-exploitation is to maintain persistent access to the compromised system. To achieve this, attackers may employ various tactics, such as creating hidden backdoors, using rootkits, and establishing covert communication channels. These techniques allow attackers to revisit the compromised system and control it over an extended period. Rootkits, in particular, are sophisticated software or hardware components that can modify the core functions of an operating system, making them extremely difficult to detect. Attackers may use rootkits to hide their presence and maintain access without arousing suspicion. Privilege escalation is another common objective during post-exploitation. Once inside a system, attackers seek to elevate their privileges to gain greater control over the compromised system. This can involve exploiting vulnerabilities, bypassing access controls, or abusing misconfigurations to gain administrative or root-level access. By escalating privileges, attackers can move laterally within a network, compromise additional systems, and access sensitive data or critical resources. Data exfiltration is a significant concern during post-exploitation. Attackers may seek to steal valuable data, such as customer information, intellectual property, or financial records. To accomplish this, they may use various methods, including exfiltrating data through hidden channels, concealing it within legitimate traffic, or compressing and encrypting it to avoid detection. Data exfiltration techniques can be highly sophisticated, making it challenging for defenders to detect and prevent. Covering tracks is another critical aspect of post-exploitation. Attackers aim to erase evidence of their presence, activities, and the methods used to compromise a system. This may involve deleting log files, altering timestamps, and manipulating audit trails to make it difficult for incident responders and forensic analysts to reconstruct the attack. On the defensive side, organizations need robust post-exploitation detection and response strategies. This includes implementing comprehensive monitoring and logging solutions, which capture detailed information about system activities and user behaviors. By analyzing these logs and applying anomaly detection algorithms, organizations can identify suspicious or unauthorized activities indicative of post-exploitation. Employing endpoint detection and response (EDR) solutions can provide real-time visibility into system and network activities, enabling rapid response to potential threats. Advanced threat hunting techniques, such as behavioral analysis and threat intelligence integration, can help security teams proactively identify post-exploitation activities. Additionally, organizations should have an incident response plan in place, outlining how to react when a post-exploitation scenario is suspected or confirmed. This plan should include steps for containing the threat, eradicating the attacker's presence, and recovering affected systems. In summary, advanced techniques for post-exploitation are essential for both attackers and defenders in the cybersecurity landscape. Attackers use these techniques to maintain access, escalate privileges, exfiltrate data, and cover their tracks, while defenders employ them to detect, respond to, and mitigate threats. Understanding these advanced techniques is critical for organizations seeking to protect their systems and data from cyber threats and breaches. By staying informed and adopting a proactive approach to post-exploitation, security professionals can better defend against evolving cyber threats. Implementing stealthy persistence mechanisms is a crucial aspect of advanced cybersecurity, allowing attackers to maintain unauthorized access to a compromised system or network while avoiding detection by security measures and defenders. These persistence mechanisms enable attackers to establish long-term control and carry out malicious activities over extended periods. In this chapter, we will explore the concept of stealthy persistence mechanisms, their importance in the realm of cybersecurity, and how they are implemented. Persistence mechanisms are a fundamental part of post-exploitation, as they help attackers ensure that their access remains undiscovered by security teams and can be maintained for as long as needed. Stealthy persistence mechanisms are designed to achieve this goal by blending in with normal system operations and evading detection by security solutions. One common method of implementing stealthy persistence is through the use of rootkits. Rootkits are a type of malicious software that can modify or replace critical components of an operating system to hide the presence of an attacker. By altering system functions and APIs, rootkits can intercept and manipulate system calls, effectively concealing malicious activities. Another technique involves leveraging legitimate system services or scheduled tasks to establish persistence. Attackers can schedule malicious scripts or executables to run at specific times or in response to system events, making it challenging to distinguish their actions from normal system activities. Fileless malware is another example of stealthy persistence. Fileless malware operates in memory, leaving no traces on the file system, making it harder to detect through traditional antivirus solutions. Memory-resident malware can execute malicious code directly from RAM, making it challenging for security tools to identify and remove it. Kernel-level exploits can also be used to achieve stealthy persistence. These exploits target vulnerabilities in the operating system's kernel, providing attackers with elevated privileges and the ability to manipulate the system at a deep level. Once exploited, these vulnerabilities allow attackers to maintain control over the system even after reboots or security updates. Steganography is yet another method used to implement stealthy persistence. Steganography involves hiding malicious code or data within legitimate files or communications. By concealing their activities within innocuous-looking files, attackers can avoid arousing suspicion. Establishing covert communication channels is a critical aspect of stealthy persistence. Attackers need a way to interact with the compromised system without raising red flags. They often use covert channels, which are communication methods that blend with normal network traffic or use non-standard protocols. These channels enable attackers to send and receive commands and exfiltrate data without detection. Tunneling over DNS, covert timing channels, or even utilizing uncommon ports and protocols are examples of techniques used to establish covert communication. Implementing stealthy persistence mechanisms requires a deep understanding of operating systems, network protocols, and security measures. Attackers often conduct thorough reconnaissance to identify vulnerabilities and weaknesses in their target systems before deploying persistence mechanisms. On the defensive side, organizations must employ advanced threat detection and response strategies to identify and mitigate stealthy persistence mechanisms effectively. This includes continuous monitoring of system and network activities, the use of behavioral analytics to detect anomalies, and regular vulnerability assessments to identify potential entry points for attackers. Security teams should also stay informed about emerging threats and tactics used by attackers to implement stealthy persistence. Ultimately, preventing and countering stealthy persistence mechanisms requires a multi-layered approach to security that combines technology, processes, and skilled professionals. In summary, implementing stealthy persistence mechanisms is a critical component of post-exploitation activities in the world of cybersecurity. Attackers use various techniques, such as rootkits, fileless malware, and covert communication channels, to ensure their access remains undetected. On the defensive side, organizations must invest in advanced security solutions and maintain a proactive stance to detect and mitigate these stealthy threats effectively. By understanding the methods employed by attackers and staying vigilant, security professionals can better protect their systems and networks from stealthy persistence mechanisms and maintain a strong defense against evolving cyber threats.

Chapter 8: Wireless Network Auditing and Assessment Tools

Comprehensive wireless network auditing tools are essential for security professionals, administrators, and ethical hackers to assess the security of wireless networks thoroughly. These tools help identify vulnerabilities and weaknesses in Wi-Fi networks, allowing organizations to strengthen their defenses and protect against potential threats. In this chapter, we will explore a range of comprehensive wireless network auditing tools and their key features. One widely used tool for wireless network auditing is Aircrack-ng, which is a suite of tools designed for assessing Wi-Fi security. Aircrack-ng can capture and analyze Wi-Fi packets, crack WEP and WPA keys, and perform various attacks to test network security. It supports a wide range of wireless network adapters and is available for both Linux and Windows operating systems. Wireshark, a popular network protocol analyzer, can also be utilized for wireless network auditing. It allows users to capture and inspect wireless traffic, making it useful for troubleshooting network issues and identifying potential security threats. Wireshark supports various Wi-Fi-related protocols and can decode encrypted traffic if the encryption keys are available. Kismet is another powerful tool for wireless network auditing, specifically designed for network sniffing and monitoring. It can passively discover and log Wi-Fi networks in the vicinity, including hidden SSIDs, and provides detailed information about the networks, such as encryption types and signal strength. Kismet is available for multiple platforms and can work with various wireless network adapters. When it comes to assessing the security of Wi-Fi passwords, tools like Hashcat can be invaluable. Hashcat is a robust password recovery tool that supports a wide range of hash algorithms, including those used in Wi-Fi encryption. Security professionals can use Hashcat to perform brute-force and dictionary attacks to crack Wi-Fi passwords, helping identify weak and vulnerable network access points. In addition to these tools, Reaver is a specialized tool for auditing Wi-Fi networks that use the WPS (Wi-Fi Protected Setup) feature. Reaver can exploit vulnerabilities in WPS implementations to recover WPA/WPA2 keys and gain unauthorized access to networks. It automates the process of attacking WPS-enabled routers and can be a valuable tool for penetration testers. Another tool worth mentioning is Fern Wi-Fi Cracker, which is a graphical user interface (GUI) tool designed for auditing wireless networks. Fern provides an intuitive interface for tasks like scanning for networks, capturing packets, and cracking Wi-Fi keys. It simplifies the auditing process and is suitable for users who may not be as comfortable with command-line tools. For professionals seeking an all-in-one solution for wireless network auditing, the WiFi Pineapple is a hardware-based tool that combines various features and functionalities. It can act as a rogue access point, intercept and manipulate network traffic, and perform man-in-the-middle attacks. The WiFi Pineapple is particularly useful for conducting penetration tests and security assessments on Wi-Fi networks. Wifite is a Python script that automates wireless network auditing tasks, making it a convenient choice for both beginners and experienced users. It can target WEP, WPA, and WPS networks and supports several attack methods, such as deauthentication and dictionary attacks. Wifite simplifies the process of auditing and cracking Wi-Fi passwords, saving time and effort. In addition to these tools, organizations should also consider using hardware-based wireless intrusion detection and prevention systems (WIDS/WIPS) to enhance their network security. These systems can actively monitor and protect Wi-Fi networks by detecting and responding to suspicious activities and unauthorized access attempts. While these comprehensive wireless network auditing tools are valuable for assessing and enhancing Wi-Fi security, it's crucial to use them responsibly and ethically. Unauthorized and malicious use of these tools can lead to legal consequences and harm to individuals or organizations. Security professionals should always obtain proper authorization and permissions before conducting any network audits or penetration tests. In summary, comprehensive wireless network auditing tools play a crucial role in assessing and improving the security of Wi-Fi networks. These tools, such as Aircrack-ng, Wireshark, Kismet, Hashcat, Reaver, Fern Wi-Fi Cracker, WiFi Pineapple, and Wifite, offer a wide range of capabilities for security professionals and ethical hackers. When used responsibly and with the necessary permissions, these tools can help identify vulnerabilities, secure wireless networks, and protect against potential threats. Security practitioners should stay informed about the latest tools and techniques in the field to effectively safeguard Wi-Fi networks in an ever-evolving threat landscape. In the realm of Wi-Fi assessment and security testing, advanced features and customization options are essential for tailoring assessments to specific requirements and gaining deeper insights into the security posture of wireless networks. These advanced capabilities extend beyond the basic functions provided by standard Wi-Fi assessment tools, allowing security professionals and ethical hackers to perform more comprehensive and specialized assessments. One such advanced feature is the ability to perform targeted attacks on wireless networks to identify vulnerabilities and weaknesses. Tools like Aircrack-ng and Wireshark offer advanced options for capturing and analyzing Wi-Fi traffic, enabling security practitioners to focus on specific network segments or devices. This targeted approach can help identify security issues more efficiently, allowing for more effective remediation. Customization in Wi-Fi assessment tools often includes the ability to fine-tune scanning and monitoring parameters. For example, professionals can adjust the scanning frequency and intensity to minimize network disruption during assessments. This level of customization is crucial when conducting security assessments in production environments where network downtime must be avoided. Another aspect of customization is the ability to select specific attack methods and techniques based on the target network's characteristics. This level of granularity allows testers to tailor their approach to the network's security measures, increasing the likelihood of successful vulnerability identification. Advanced tools also offer extensive customization of attack payloads and parameters. For example, password-cracking tools like Hashcat provide options to create custom wordlists and rule sets, increasing the chances of cracking complex Wi-Fi passwords. Similarly, wireless assessment tools such as

Wifite and Fern Wi-Fi Cracker allow users to customize attack profiles, specifying the type of attacks to perform and the order in which they should be executed. Customization also extends to reporting and result interpretation. Advanced tools often provide flexible reporting options, enabling users to generate detailed reports that align with their organization's specific requirements. These reports can include information on vulnerabilities, recommendations for remediation, and even compliance-related data. Furthermore, customization allows security professionals to tailor the reporting format and level of detail to meet the needs of different stakeholders, such as executives, IT teams, or regulatory bodies. Beyond customization, advanced features in Wi-Fi assessment tools often include integration with other security tools and platforms. This integration can streamline workflows by allowing data sharing and collaboration across different security solutions. For instance, some tools offer integration with vulnerability management systems, ensuring that identified Wi-Fi vulnerabilities are seamlessly incorporated into an organization's overall risk management process. Additionally, integration with threat intelligence feeds can enhance the accuracy of assessments by providing real-time information about emerging threats and vulnerabilities. Another advanced feature is the ability to perform in-depth analysis of Wi-Fi encryption protocols and authentication mechanisms. Advanced tools can dissect the inner workings of encryption protocols like WEP, WPA, and WPA2/WPA3, helping security professionals identify potential weaknesses and misconfigurations. This level of analysis is crucial for understanding the security of Wi-Fi networks and ensuring that they meet industry best practices. Moreover, advanced tools can simulate more sophisticated attacks, such as man-in-the-middle (MITM) attacks or rogue access point attacks. These simulations can help organizations assess their resilience to advanced threats and understand how attackers might exploit vulnerabilities in their Wi-Fi infrastructure. Customization also extends to scripting and automation capabilities within Wi-Fi assessment tools. Many advanced tools support scripting languages like Python, allowing users to create custom scripts for specific tasks or automate repetitive assessment processes. Automation can significantly increase efficiency, especially when performing large-scale or ongoing assessments of multiple Wi-Fi networks. Advanced Wi-Fi assessment tools often provide detailed visualizations and mapping capabilities. These features allow security professionals to create comprehensive network maps, visualize signal strength, and identify the physical locations of access points. Visualization is instrumental in understanding network topologies and planning security measures effectively. Additionally, some tools offer real-time monitoring and alerting capabilities, enabling security teams to detect and respond to suspicious activities or unauthorized access attempts promptly. This proactive approach can help organizations mitigate security threats before they escalate. When considering advanced features and customization in Wi-Fi assessment tools, it's essential to strike a balance between flexibility and complexity. While advanced tools offer a wide range of capabilities, they may require a steeper learning curve and a deeper understanding of Wi-Fi technologies and security concepts. Organizations should invest in training and skill development for their security teams to maximize the benefits of these advanced tools. Furthermore, it's crucial to keep abreast of updates and new features introduced by tool developers to leverage the latest advancements in Wi-Fi assessment and security testing. In summary, advanced features and customization options are pivotal in the field of Wi-Fi assessment and security testing. These capabilities empower security professionals and ethical hackers to tailor their assessments, target vulnerabilities efficiently, and gain deeper insights into the security of wireless networks. Customization extends to scanning parameters, attack techniques, reporting formats, and integration with other security tools. Additionally, advanced tools offer in-depth analysis of encryption protocols, automation capabilities, visualization, and real-time monitoring. Balancing flexibility with complexity is essential, and organizations should invest in training to harness the full potential of these advanced Wi-Fi assessment tools. By leveraging these capabilities, organizations can enhance their Wi-Fi security posture and protect against evolving threats in the wireless landscape.

Chapter 9: Insider Threats and Advanced Social Engineering

Recognizing and mitigating insider threats is a critical aspect of modern cybersecurity practices, as these threats pose unique challenges to organizations. Insider threats, unlike external threats, come from individuals within the organization who have privileged access and knowledge of its systems and data. These individuals can be employees, contractors, or business partners, making it challenging to distinguish them from legitimate users. Insider threats can be intentional or unintentional, and they encompass a wide range of behaviors and motivations. One common category of insider threat is the malicious insider, someone within the organization who intentionally seeks to harm it. Motivations for these individuals can include financial gain, revenge, ideology, or even simple mischief. Malicious insiders often have the knowledge and access needed to carry out significant attacks, making them a potent danger. Another type of insider threat is the negligent or careless insider, someone who inadvertently compromises security due to their actions or negligence. This could involve mishandling sensitive data, falling victim to phishing attacks, or failing to follow security protocols. Negligent insiders can unknowingly expose the organization to risks, emphasizing the importance of security awareness training. To recognize and mitigate insider threats effectively, organizations must adopt a multifaceted approach. One key element is the development and implementation of robust security policies and procedures. These policies should clearly define acceptable use of IT resources, access controls, and data handling procedures. Employees should be educated about these policies and regularly reminded of their importance.

Access control plays a critical role in mitigating insider threats. Organizations should employ the principle of least privilege, ensuring that employees only have access to the resources and data necessary for their roles. Access should be regularly reviewed and revoked when no longer needed. Another critical aspect is monitoring and auditing user activities. This involves keeping a close eye on network traffic, system logs, and user behavior. Anomalies or suspicious activities should be flagged for further investigation. Advanced threat detection tools can be employed to help automate this process and identify potential insider threats. Implementing a robust incident response plan is vital. In the event of a security incident involving an insider threat, organizations should have procedures in place to investigate, contain, and mitigate the threat swiftly. This plan should involve collaboration among IT, security, and legal departments. Insider threats often involve insider knowledge, which makes user training and awareness programs crucial. Employees should be educated about the various forms of insider threats, including social engineering tactics used by malicious insiders. Regular training can help employees recognize suspicious activities and report them promptly. Additionally, organizations should foster a culture of security where employees feel comfortable reporting security concerns without fear of reprisal. Background checks and thorough vetting of employees during the hiring process can also help mitigate insider threats. While this approach won't catch all potential insider threats, it can reduce the risk of hiring individuals with malicious intent. In some cases, organizations may implement user activity monitoring tools that track and record user actions on company devices and systems. These tools can help detect unusual or unauthorized activities that may indicate insider threats. However, it's essential to balance monitoring with privacy considerations and inform employees about such practices. Intrusion detection systems (IDS) and intrusion prevention systems (IPS) can be valuable tools for recognizing insider threats. These systems can analyze network traffic and system logs to identify suspicious patterns or behaviors that may indicate an insider threat. They can also block or alert on such activities in real-time, helping to mitigate risks. Organizations should establish an incident response team that includes representatives from IT, security, legal, and human resources departments. This team should be trained and prepared to respond swiftly and effectively to insider threat incidents. A well-structured response can help contain the threat and prevent further damage. Regular security audits and assessments are essential for identifying and mitigating insider threats. These assessments should include penetration testing, vulnerability scanning, and review of access controls and policies. By regularly evaluating the security posture of the organization, weaknesses and vulnerabilities can be addressed proactively. Data loss prevention (DLP) solutions can help protect sensitive data from insider threats by monitoring and controlling data flows within the organization. These solutions can prevent unauthorized access, sharing, or transmission of sensitive information. Encryption should be employed to protect data at rest and in transit, making it more challenging for insiders to access sensitive information. User behavior analytics (UBA) tools can help organizations detect unusual or suspicious behavior patterns among their employees. These tools use machine learning and behavioral analysis to identify potential insider threats based on deviations from normal behavior. In addition to technical measures, organizations should promote a culture of trust and open communication. Employees should feel comfortable reporting security concerns or incidents without fear of retaliation. This transparency can help identify and address insider threats more effectively. Recognizing and mitigating insider threats is an ongoing process that requires a combination of technical controls, policies and procedures, employee education, and proactive monitoring. By adopting a multifaceted approach, organizations can better protect themselves from the diverse and evolving threats that insiders may pose. Overall, the key to mitigating insider threats lies in a combination of proactive prevention, effective detection, and swift response when incidents occur. Advanced social engineering tactics in Wi-Fi attacks represent a significant threat to individuals and organizations, as attackers continue to evolve their methods to manipulate human behavior. Social engineering relies on psychological manipulation to deceive individuals into revealing sensitive information, granting access, or taking specific actions. In Wi-Fi attacks, social engineering can be particularly effective due to the widespread use of wireless networks and the inherent trust users place in them. Attackers leverage various advanced tactics to exploit this trust and compromise Wi-Fi networks. One common advanced social engineering tactic is pretexting, where the attacker creates a fabricated scenario or pretext to manipulate the victim into divulging information or taking specific actions. For example, an attacker may impersonate a trusted IT technician and call an employee, claiming they need to troubleshoot a Wi-Fi issue. The attacker then convinces the employee to provide network credentials or other sensitive information. Pretexting relies on social engineering skills and the ability to build rapport and credibility with the target. Phishing remains a prevalent social engineering tactic in Wi-Fi attacks, but advanced phishing techniques have emerged. Spear phishing, for instance, targets specific individuals or organizations with highly tailored and convincing messages. Attackers research their targets extensively, often using publicly available information to craft personalized emails or messages. These messages appear legitimate and entice victims to click on malicious links or download malicious attachments, compromising their devices and potentially the entire network. Another variant, known as whaling, focuses on high-profile targets like executives or individuals with access to sensitive information. Attackers impersonate trusted entities or individuals in these messages, increasing the likelihood of success. Vishing, or voice phishing, is an advanced social engineering tactic that involves using phone calls to deceive victims. Attackers may impersonate legitimate organizations, government agencies, or tech support services to extract sensitive information or gain remote access to the victim's device. Smishing combines SMS or text messaging with phishing techniques, where victims receive fake messages with malicious links or requests for personal information. To counter advanced social engineering tactics, individuals and organizations should prioritize security awareness and education. Training programs can help employees recognize suspicious requests or messages and teach them how to verify the legitimacy of communications. Multi-factor authentication (MFA) should be implemented wherever possible to provide an additional layer of security, making it more challenging for attackers to compromise accounts even if credentials are stolen. Organizations can employ email filtering and content inspection tools to detect and block phishing attempts. Advanced threat detection solutions that use machine learning and behavioral analysis can identify abnormal or suspicious user behavior, helping to detect social engineering attacks. Using strong, unique passwords and password managers can reduce the risk of successful attacks.

Employees should be encouraged to use complex passwords and avoid password reuse across accounts. Endpoint security solutions can help protect individual devices from malware and malicious attachments often delivered through social engineering attacks. Regularly updating software and operating systems is crucial, as many social engineering attacks exploit known vulnerabilities. Implementing strict access controls and network segmentation can limit the impact of successful attacks by preventing lateral movement within the network. Advanced social engineering tactics in Wi-Fi attacks are continually evolving, making it imperative for individuals and organizations to remain vigilant. By staying informed about these tactics, implementing security best practices, and fostering a culture of cybersecurity awareness, it's possible to mitigate the risks associated with social engineering and protect both personal and organizational assets. In an increasingly digital world, where Wi-Fi networks play a pivotal role in connectivity, safeguarding against advanced social engineering tactics is paramount to maintaining security and trust.

Chapter 10: Defending Against Nation-State-Level Attacks

Understanding nation-state threat actors is crucial in the realm of cybersecurity, as these entities pose some of the most sophisticated and potent challenges to the security of nations, organizations, and individuals. Nation-state threat actors, also known as advanced persistent threats (APTs), are typically state-sponsored or state-affiliated groups that conduct cyber-espionage, cyber-sabotage, and cyber-warfare operations on behalf of a nation or government. These threat actors operate with significant resources, including skilled hackers, advanced technology, and substantial financial backing. Their primary objectives can range from stealing sensitive government or corporate data to disrupting critical infrastructure or conducting cyber-espionage to advance national interests. One fundamental characteristic of nation-state threat actors is their persistence. They often engage in long-term campaigns, infiltrating target systems and maintaining a low profile to avoid detection for extended periods. This persistence allows them to gather intelligence, monitor adversaries, and execute attacks when the timing is most advantageous. Attribution of attacks to nation-state threat actors can be complex, as they employ various techniques to obfuscate their origins. They may use proxy servers, compromised systems in other countries, or even launch attacks from within the victim's own country, making it appear as if the attack originated locally. The motivations of nation-state threat actors can vary widely based on the specific goals and interests of the sponsoring nation. Some may focus on economic espionage, stealing intellectual property and trade secrets to gain a competitive advantage in global markets. Others may engage in cyber-espionage to collect information for political or military purposes, such as understanding the intentions and capabilities of rival nations. Cyber-sabotage is another facet of nation-state threat actor activities, involving the disruption or destruction of critical infrastructure, including power grids, transportation systems, or financial institutions. This type of cyber-attack can have severe real-world consequences and is a growing concern for national security. Understanding the tactics, techniques, and procedures (TTPs) employed by nation-state threat actors is essential for effective defense. These actors often use advanced malware, zero-day vulnerabilities, and sophisticated social engineering tactics to compromise their targets. They may exploit known vulnerabilities, but they are also known for discovering and exploiting previously unknown vulnerabilities. Their malware is typically custom-built or highly modified to avoid detection by antivirus software and other security measures. Moreover, they often employ "living off the land" techniques, using legitimate tools and processes already present on the victim's network to move laterally and maintain persistence. To defend against nation-state threat actors, organizations and governments must adopt a proactive and multi-layered security approach. This includes continuous monitoring and threat hunting to detect suspicious activities and anomalies within the network. Regular security assessments and penetration testing can help identify vulnerabilities that might be exploited by these actors. Additionally, organizations should implement robust access controls, network segmentation, and strong authentication mechanisms to limit the impact of potential breaches. Information sharing and collaboration with other organizations and government agencies can provide valuable threat intelligence to identify and respond to nation-state threats more effectively. Education and training of personnel are also essential components of defense, as security awareness can help prevent successful social engineering attacks. Governments play a crucial role in addressing nation-state threat actors by developing and enforcing cybersecurity policies and regulations. They should invest in national cyber defense capabilities and establish clear guidelines for incident response and reporting. International cooperation is essential to address the global nature of these threats, as nation-state actors often operate across borders. Efforts to establish norms of responsible state behavior in cyberspace can help mitigate the risks of cyber-conflict. Finally, attribution of cyber-attacks to nation-state threat actors is a complex and politically sensitive process. Multiple factors, including technical indicators, open-source intelligence, and classified information, are considered to identify the responsible party. Publicly attributing an attack can have diplomatic consequences, and governments must weigh the risks and benefits carefully. In summary, understanding nation-state threat actors and their tactics is essential for effective cybersecurity. These actors, often well-funded and highly skilled, pose significant challenges to governments, organizations, and individuals. Their objectives range from espionage and theft of intellectual property to cyber-sabotage and disruption of critical infrastructure. Detecting and defending against nation-state threats require a proactive and multi-layered approach, including robust cybersecurity measures, information sharing, and international cooperation. While attribution can be complex and politically sensitive, it is a critical step in holding threat actors accountable for their actions and deterring future attacks. By staying informed and vigilant, individuals and organizations can contribute to a safer and more secure digital environment. In the ever-evolving landscape of cybersecurity, advanced defensive strategies and countermeasures are essential for protecting against a wide range of threats. These strategies go beyond traditional security measures and are designed to mitigate the risks posed by sophisticated adversaries, such as nation-state actors and highly skilled hackers. One key aspect of advanced defensive strategies is proactive threat hunting, where security teams actively seek out signs of compromise within their networks. Rather than relying solely on automated security tools, threat hunters use their expertise to identify unusual or suspicious activities that may indicate a breach. This approach helps organizations detect and respond to threats more quickly, reducing the potential impact of an attack. Another critical component of advanced defense is the use of deception technology. Deception tools create decoy assets within a network that mimic real systems and data, enticing attackers to interact with them. By luring adversaries into these decoy environments, organizations can gather valuable threat intelligence and gain insight into the tactics, techniques, and procedures (TTPs) of their adversaries. Furthermore, deception technology can delay attackers, allowing defenders more time to respond effectively. Machine learning and artificial intelligence (AI) are increasingly used in advanced defensive strategies to augment human capabilities. These technologies can analyze vast amounts of data and identify patterns or anomalies that may not be apparent to human analysts. AI-driven security tools can detect and respond to threats in real-time, helping organizations stay ahead of rapidly evolving cyber threats. Network segmentation is a fundamental element of advanced defensive strategies. By dividing a network into isolated segments, organizations can contain the spread of malware and limit an attacker's lateral movement. This approach minimizes the potential damage that an intruder can inflict and enhances overall network security. Zero Trust Architecture (ZTA) is another critical concept in advanced defense. ZTA assumes that threats may exist both outside and inside the network and, as such, requires continuous verification of user identity and device integrity. Access to resources is restricted to the minimum necessary, reducing the attack surface and ensuring that only authorized users and devices can access sensitive data. Continuous monitoring and real-time threat detection are essential for advanced defensive strategies. Security Information and Event Management (SIEM) systems, combined with User and Entity Behavior Analytics (UEBA), provide organizations with the ability to detect and respond to security incidents as they occur. These tools analyze network traffic, user behavior, and system logs to identify suspicious activities and potential security breaches. Moreover, incident response planning is a crucial element of advanced defense. Organizations should have well-defined incident response plans in place, detailing how to react to various types of security incidents. These plans include procedures for containing and mitigating the incident, communicating with stakeholders, and restoring normal operations. Collaboration and information sharing within the cybersecurity community play a vital role in advanced defense. Threat intelligence sharing enables organizations to benefit from the collective knowledge of the cybersecurity community, helping them stay informed about emerging threats and attack techniques. Participation in Information Sharing and Analysis Centers (ISACs) and other industry-specific groups can provide access to valuable threat intelligence. Red teaming and penetration testing are proactive approaches used in advanced defensive strategies. These practices involve ethical hackers simulating real-world attacks to identify vulnerabilities and weaknesses in an organization's defenses. By emulating the tactics of adversaries, organizations can better understand their security posture and take steps to address any weaknesses. Security awareness training is an ongoing process that helps employees recognize and respond to potential security threats. Aware and well-informed employees can be a critical line of defense against phishing attacks, social engineering, and other threats that target human vulnerabilities. The principle of least privilege is fundamental to advanced defense. It ensures that users, applications, and systems have only the minimum level of access and permissions required to perform their tasks. This limits the potential impact of a security breach and reduces the attack surface. Regularly patching and updating software and systems is a basic yet essential aspect of advanced defense. Vulnerabilities in outdated software can be exploited by attackers, making it crucial to stay up to date with security patches and updates. Advanced defense strategies also involve proactive threat intelligence gathering. This includes monitoring underground forums, tracking emerging threats, and studying the tactics of specific threat actors. By gaining insights into the motivations and capabilities of potential adversaries, organizations can better prepare for and defend against cyber-attacks. Intrusion detection and prevention systems (IDS/IPS) are key components of advanced defense. These systems continuously monitor network traffic and can automatically block or alert on suspicious activities. They provide an additional layer of security that can help organizations detect and respond to threats in real-time. Encryption and data protection are crucial for safeguarding sensitive information. Advanced defense strategies often include end-to-end encryption, data loss prevention (DLP) solutions, and robust access controls. These measures ensure that even if an attacker gains access to data, it remains unreadable and unusable. Advanced defensive strategies also consider the insider threat. While external threats are a significant concern, organizations must be vigilant regarding the potential risks posed by employees, contractors, or partners with malicious intent or inadvertently compromising security. In summary, advanced defensive strategies and countermeasures are essential in today's complex cybersecurity landscape. These strategies encompass proactive threat hunting, deception technology, machine learning, network segmentation, and a Zero Trust Architecture. Continuous monitoring, incident response planning, and collaboration within the cybersecurity community are also crucial elements. Red teaming, security awareness training, and the principle of least privilege play important roles in strengthening defenses. By adopting these advanced defense measures, organizations can better protect their assets and data against a wide range of cyber threats.

Conclusion

In the realm of cybersecurity, where the battle between defenders and adversaries rages on, knowledge is the most potent weapon. This book bundle, titled "Wireless Security Masterclass: Penetration Testing for Network Defenders and Ethical Hackers," has provided readers with a comprehensive and in-depth exploration of wireless network security and penetration testing.

In Book 1, "Wireless Network Security Essentials: A Beginner's Guide," we embarked on a journey through the fundamentals of wireless security. We built a strong foundation, learning about encryption, authentication, and the various security protocols that protect our wireless networks. This book catered to beginners, equipping them with essential knowledge to secure their networks effectively.

Book 2, "Hacking Wi-Fi Networks: Intermediate Techniques for Penetration Testers," took us deeper into the world of wireless security. Here, we explored the techniques employed by ethical hackers and penetration testers to uncover vulnerabilities in Wi-Fi networks. We delved into more advanced topics such as cracking Wi-Fi passwords and conducting wireless reconnaissance. This intermediate guide empowered readers to take their penetration testing skills to the next level.

Book 3, "Advanced Wireless Exploitation: A Comprehensive Guide to Penetration Testing," elevated our understanding further. We dived into the intricacies of wireless exploitation, dissecting advanced attacks and defenses. Readers learned how to identify hidden SSIDs, exploit weaknesses in Wi-Fi protocols, and evade intrusion detection systems. This book equipped readers with the knowledge and skills required to conduct comprehensive penetration tests on wireless networks.

Finally, Book 4, "Wireless Network Mastery: Expert-Level Penetration Testing and Defense," marked the pinnacle of our journey. Here, we explored expert-level penetration testing techniques, advanced network mapping, and the art of exploiting misconfigurations. Additionally, we covered the critical aspects of maintaining persistent access, anti-forensic techniques, and countermeasures for detection and attribution. This book transformed readers into seasoned experts capable of defending against the most sophisticated wireless attacks.

As we conclude this "Wireless Security Masterclass" book bundle, we must recognize the significance of the knowledge gained. With the ever-evolving threat landscape, the skills and insights acquired from these four books are invaluable. Readers are now well-equipped to protect their own networks, engage in ethical hacking, and secure the wireless world around us.

In the ongoing battle between network defenders and adversaries, this book bundle serves as a beacon of education, promoting ethical hacking practices and enhancing cybersecurity. Whether you are a novice seeking to establish a strong security foundation or an expert looking to sharpen your penetration testing skills, this bundle has something to offer.

With the knowledge imparted in these books, readers have the power to fortify their defenses, identify vulnerabilities, and contribute to the collective effort of making our wireless world a safer place. Remember, in the world of wireless security, knowledge truly is power, and this "Wireless Security Masterclass" book bundle has bestowed that power upon you. May you wield it responsibly and ethically, ensuring the security of networks far and wide.

www.ingramcontent.com/pod-product-compliance
Lightning Source LLC
Chambersburg PA
CBHW071236050326
40690CB00011B/2148